PROTOTYPE 4

(2022)

CONTENTS

Natalie Linh Bolderston (4–7)
- Visitation
- Slaughter
- Love Poem in a Safe City

J. R. Carpenter (8–9)
- furies
- now you know

Yannis Ritsos (trans. Paul Merchant) & Chiara Ambrosio (10–13)
- from *Linocut Monochords*

Nathan Dragon (14–17)
- from *FUG*

Hao Guang Tse (18–19)
- as like hives of meaning, buzzing & not quite stable
- which is when charcoal was passed from her body to mine

Nancy Campbell (20–21)
- filaments

Sascha Akhtar (22–23)
- The Butterfly Sanctuary

Eve Esfandiari-Denney (24–27)
- Solo to bird phoenix
- what vultures are singing
- After Leyly

Jack Barker-Clark (28–32)
- Cowl

Emily Cooper & Jo Burns (33–39)
- from *The Conversation*

Alan Fielden (40–41)
- from *Container*

ajw (42–45)
- Sink In / III

Laura Elliott (46–53)
- Sprawl Song

Chrissy Williams (54–57)
- Congruence

Jay Gao (58–63)
- Body Sonnet

Martha Kapos (64–66)
- Impromptu
- Instrument

Xuela Zhang (67–69)
- Quarantine I
- Quarantine II
- Translator's Note III

Scott Thurston (70–73)
- from *FAILSAFE*

Rory Cook (74–75)
- Of Imitation
- Useless Setting

Ralf Webb (76–87)
- Dark Wood

Kate Crowcroft (88–91)
- DOOM
- RE. TRAINING
- YOUR MOTHER'S RIB BREAKS

Charlie Baylis (92–93)
- come as you are
- inner-peace necklace

Clare Fisher (94–95)
- WTAF

Samra Mayanja (96–98)
- SCREAM

Honor Gareth Gavin (99–105)
- A Self-Made Man?

Joe Carrick-Varty (106–111)
- from *sky doc*

Emily Hasler (112–113)
- Course
- A Mud

Edward Doegar (114–118)
- from *I never thought it would come to this*

Victoria Manifold (119–124)
- Daytrippers

Robert Casselton Clark (125–128)
- from *Scripts*

Jessa Mockridge (129–141)
- SWIM

fred spoliar (142–144)
- Rosé

Kimberly Reyes (145–147)
- The foundation is likely beyond repair
- corralled to complicit
- Don't Let it Trouble Your Mind

Livia Franchini (148–149)
- An Abundance
- The Professor

Annie Katchinska (150–153)
- Fructose

Rochelle Roberts (154–157)
- ∞
- †
- ~
- ±

Sam Weselowski (158–162)
- from *Triple Rainforest*

Grace Henes (163–169)
- Machines of Loving Grace

Helen Palmer (170–178)
- from *Pleasure Beach*

Alisha Dietzman (179–182)
- Love Poem by the Light of Eternity and a Reality TV Show About Love
- Untitled, Spring
- COMMENTS ON AN ARTICLE ABOUT THE SARCO SUICIDE POD: THREE TRANSLATIONS
- Coda

Contributor Biographies (184–191)

Natalie Linh Bolderston

—

Visitation

Give me white fire to walk through,
    the rain
        glazed into a fisheye.
Give me the sky lying down
    in its own bright waste.
        Give me tendons and intestines,
streaks of fat that shrink to coal
    at my lips.
    Give your coal as well.
Give me chopstick wrappers,
    sachet preservatives, the licked edge
    of your cup.
Give me your roughest cloth,
    rotting elastic, the stains of loving.
Give me fever, tarred lungs, an infected tooth.
    Pain, too, can be a feast.
    Give me a photograph
of someone who has never said my name,
    never dropped coins
        into a stiff mouth.
See how my neck thins
    when the living forget,
        how I shudder at the knee.
Give me the daughter
    gathering black shells from the beach.
        (A shell is also a ghost.)
    Let me touch her nose, which is my nose,
her scarred jaw, her strange hair
    that holds the shape of English wind.
        A girl like her is always a bridge.
Graft me to her throat and ask her
        to eat for me.

Slaughter

The goddess teaches us that a woman in labour
can always smell what is in your blood.

We pray to her on days when we must be
as meatless as the spirits we feed.
We hide the knives, suck peeling skin
from cuticles and mosquito bites.

> *Disguised as a pregnant mortal*
> *I found the butcher on the riverbank,*
> *listened for the lives*
> *that still scratched at his throat.*
>
> *I let my waters break.*
> *He eyed the stains on my robes,*
> *my body as round as the pig*
> *he had slashed and hooked.*

My mother says,
If I translate this for you, will I cut my own neck?
I learn how some ghosts swell like winter gourds,
how their scalps and tongues ignite.
How they starve to atone, lick the ankles
of those who wade through water.

> *I revealed my face, freed orange light from my hair.*
> *He wept, cut himself open to wash away his wrongs.*
> *The river singed at the touch of his stomach,*
> *his body's unsnarling cords.*

My mother once dropped a bucket
of live eels at the market,
could never eat anything
that had moved against her hand.

> *The sky red and gnawable. The clouds skewered*
> *like pork belly. His viscera reborn*
> *as a venomous turtle and snake.*

I used to eat only wings and fins,
believing I would leave the rest alive.

I heard of a girl who wished to shed herself,
who opened the net around her bed each night
and invited mosquitoes to feed.

> *I took pity, showed him how to raise a blade*
> *to end his flame-eyed second life.*

My mother picks a bone from my teeth.
If we wear slaughter on our bodies,
her blessings will not touch us.

(

Love Poem in a Safe City

The hour when I watch your hands burn blue
and everything folds over the rim of touch.

You tell me we are both consequences of the sea,
its fractured mercies.

We scour this water-edged city, picking out our memorials –
the Chinatown arch; the birds chained to clocktowers.

You reveal the pulpy ache in your chest,
your feather allergy, all the ways I could kill you.

Once, we sat at the golden hem of a goddess
and named her in two languages.

We cupped her blessings like tiny fish,
carried them through airports, back to this blue-dusk room

where we question our skin, its fugitive history.
Where we anchor ourselves at high tide, calf over calf,

an island the shape of two lungs.

J. R. Carpenter
—
furies

I am not an island
swallow ship demon
not so fast easy
to chart name
measure me
type cast me
away aside adrift ashore
nor am I lit
by gas star or far
moon light alight
a light atop a foremast
turned on or off at
will this sea rise
rage see me
(through these
wind wave
wing thick
fog furies

now you know

I have acquired the habit
of making words for myself

now that I have a language
of my own

a fluid language
without suffixes

prefixes
or roots

I make feminine words
masculine

the sea, the earth
and the night   )

have become beings
of another sex than mine

my notes are written with pencil
the marks of which are not liable

to be effaced by sea-water
and because ink evaporates

it's not true
that I kissed a platypus

I rummaged through her pockets
and found nothing

now you know
everything

**Yannis Ritsos (trans. Paul Merchant)
& Chiara Ambrosio**
—

from *Linocut Monochords*

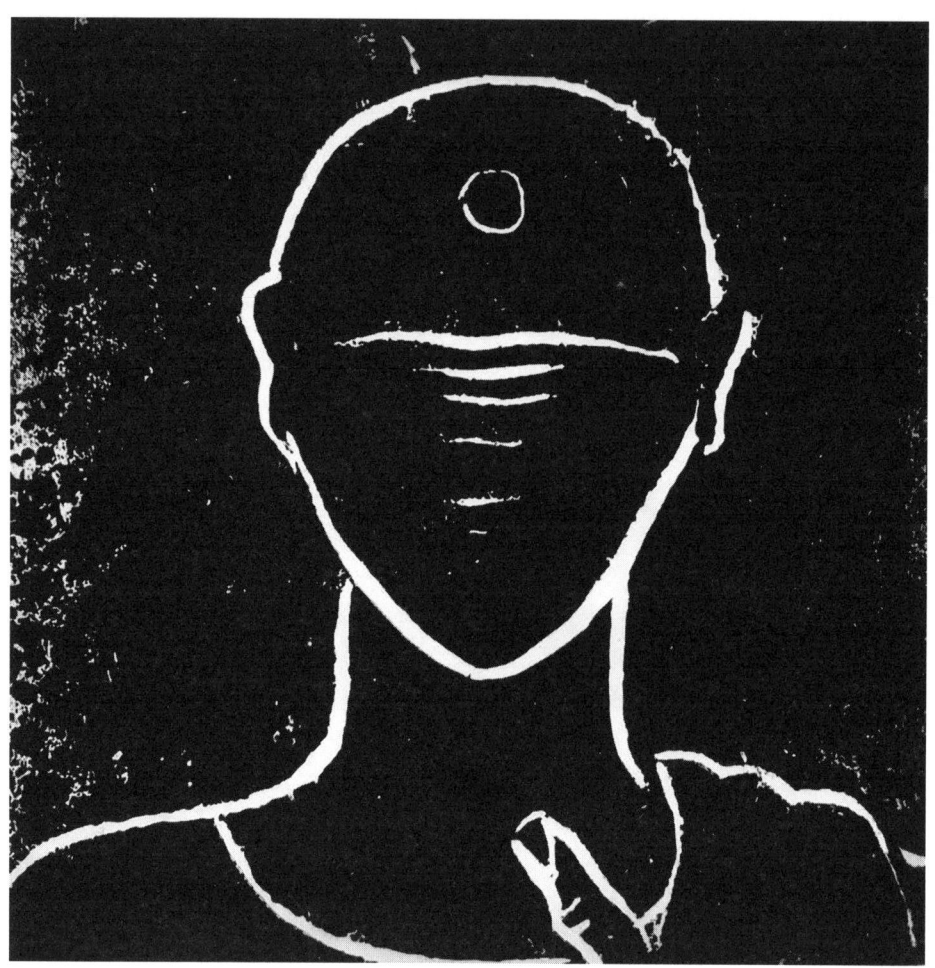

(

I saw you and remembered poems.

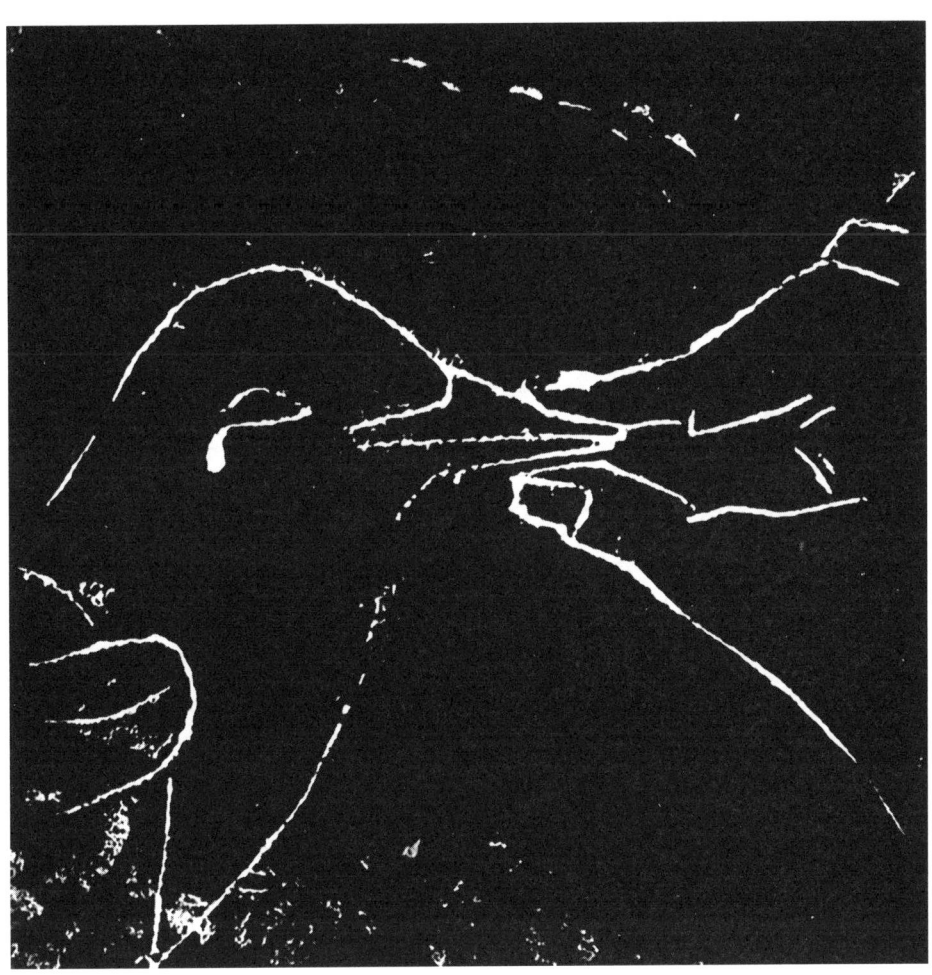

The ones stealing from you call you thief.

Yannis Ritsos (trans. Paul Merchant) & Chiara Ambrosio

(

The poem has sense, you say. Does it have a body?

Don't be afraid. Where they are going downstream there's a river and a garden.

Nathan Dragon
—
from *FUG*

A Sound You Make With Your Mouth

Things in the sky that look like they cross paths with prop planes.
    Dandelion juice and coffee.
    A day spent trying to work out an efficient push-up routine.
    He says to himself, You'll feel better.

Nacreous

I miss the sky, he thinks, looking directly at it.
    Leftovers of two planes crossing.
    Does it look dirty today? And that's why the sun looks that way in the sky, right?
(Time to go back inside.

Ridiculous

Did you hear what he said?

Winter Songbirds

He could hear singing coming down from the top of the hill: *I don't know, it's porn, you gotta be over 18.*

Have The Feeling That

The cardinal's call is eerie today.
    He has the feeling like the dog is right behind him, looking at him, but he knows the dog's in another room.
    The fruit in a bowl on the counter is getting sun right now.
    Letting himself be provoked to avoid irritation.
    There was a snake plant in nearly every shot of that film.

Small Electrical Fire

The spectacle of the result of incompatibility, smell of static.

Laps

Another neighbour walks up and down the street, holding his Walkman up by the side of his head like a hand strap on the subway. His head is deep in a cap with his face tilted up towards the sun.
    He's not sure this neighbour has ever seen him, the way this neighbour wears his cap. It seems like any time he's seen this neighbour, the neighbour's been smiling in the light with his eyes closed.
    He's never talked to this neighbour either. He'd like to though.

Paw

A plywood floor. Lying down on it.
    If he gets up he could put the radio on.
    He stays on the floor and imagines teaching the dog to turn it on.
    Just give the radio paw.
    Right here.
    No, right here.

Memory Of A Sword

It's not a toy!

Doggerel

He used to work with this guy with a nickname.
 Ohhhh-hohhh, Ihhh tell you what man—how every story started.
 You know how I got my nickname?
 I was in the Keys spearfishing...
 He'd say to the guy he worked with, Oh yeah?
 Oh yeah brother. I came up over the reef and there it was.

Working And Watching Woodpeckers Work

He thinks everyone knows that woodpeckers' tongues internally wrap around their brains. It's nothing to know this. It prevents brain damage.
 To him, they always sound like blue jays mixed with seagulls, maybe that's wrong though.
 Seeing a woodpecker always makes him feel better. They make him feel lucky to see one.

At work he's watching one.
 Guy he's working with today asks him what he's looking at.
 Tells the guy at work, look right up there, a woodpecker. It's either a downy woodpecker or a hairy woodpecker. I can't tell. They almost look the same but one's bigger, I forget which is which.
 The guy at work says, Where?
 Right there.
 That's a woodpecker? That's not what I pictured, the guy at work says. I pictured Woody the Woodpecker.
 Yeah those ones, that kind lives around here too, they live around most of the country I think, he tells the guy at work. They're called pileated woodpeckers. They get big, like a small hawk or something.

He likes this guy at work. This guy's kind of down all the time, and pretty young, younger than him.

One day he asked the guy, Do you want my old guitar? It's missing a string, probably works fine otherwise.

From What? He Thought

He takes issue with things most people say, even if they're right. They're usually right, probably.

But I like to take issue, he thinks.
He's wrong about himself all the time.
Maybe some things.
Is that a concession?
Considering all this, he wishes he was wrong all the time.
You can't get away from it.

Binoculars)

It's just another vulture. Shit, he thought. He could've sworn it was a young golden eagle.

Hao Guang Tse

—

as like hives of meaning, buzzing & not quite stable

      I trip over on

                             the way
        to pilates a crack

                in the patella
    of the earth

continuously I
    miss a spot &   a look & all

        these appointments   just
            by not needing

(I miss the daily
    ferry daily

        my living room fills w/
    search engine

                exhaust &

shame lives
        on a landfill

    of things I miss

    STAND UP! STAND UP!

wasted time   mister
    takes more time
    to distil

which is when charcoal was passed from her body to mine

        paper laps ink

    chalk-lines extend   again
                    in the sun

      muddling through
             in search of the road
       pristine

  & reaching the sky against

             whiteness, the rough
       root skin   )

   & desiring to brush
        a solitary stroke across
between river & river

           that narrow stroke
     of road

  scratch-sheets
      luminous rock
paring her face to the pith

Nancy Campbell

—

filaments

For light pulses in waves that fly towards us so swiftly that the eye reads current as continuity, flicker as flow. The artisan of light knows where to find stillness within the wave, and he will usher darkness back into the home.

A lamp defies the hands circling the clock dial, denies the blind side of celestial spheres. When the bulb is bare its glare stops us from stumbling at the soft boundaries of furniture, it spotlights souvenirs and ornaments, reveals forms that cower and blur as the room grows dim.

The artisan's role is to bluff the passing hours, to cast doubt upon edges. He knows every way to diffuse truth through intimate space, to shield our drowsy eyes from a flame—he will wrap our small electric suns in *kōzo* like glowing halos of icy silica—and the room grows dustier when dust cannot be seen, the room grows older as shadows sag into corners, for what is a shadow if not the dirt left to us as light thins and what is filth but the torn and cast-off skin of things—

and the work he makes is simple as a song grown from the earth, listen: the bark that covers trunk and sap, the bast, peeled and pounded to pulp, then washed in winter river, shaken in a frame, and set aside to dry.

§

Flecks of gold leaf shimmer among twists of fibre—shine and spin, spin and shine—bright as yolk spots and chalaza in the albumen of an egg, each sheet fine but some still more so, as smoke is finer than the wood that fuels the fire, or mist than the water it rises from—

miso-gami chunika—*kōzo* mixed with shell powder, so light when lifted, it hardly falls again, so thin the fingers lifting ghost through the glaze—and heavier, *uda-gami koban*—*kōzo* mixed with dull white mud and old wood ash—and still heavier, *sagukawa gami*—*kōzo* mixed with cedar bark, hefty and stiff, light or dark according to the quantity of cedar.

These are the artisan's albums and from them you may choose how to disguise your night. Page after pale lunar page—all wordless, some worn and frayed, curled at the fore-edge or furred by another customer's touch or torn by one careless turn, concertina'd or crumpled—a journal of empty days and then one gorgeous anomaly: a sheet dyed with indigo from *albizia julibrissin*, the silk tree, or pink, from the *sakura*.

As with scissors and knives, clocks and mirrors, imagine a superstition against words—if all books were blank: pages to shield us from too much sight, pages with which we might carve light.

Sascha Akhtar

—

The Butterfly Sanctuary

When we began two days ago, the creature, already larger,
was completely green, like unripe fruit. We had noticed in
our food cultivation that the butterflies preferred the fledging
leaves of the Romanesco-that-may-or-may-not-be,
                                                          for their egg-laying.
Initially, we sought to protect our own investment. Our own
food. For our stomachs.
                                      We removed new eggs daily.
As the butterflies persisted, laying their eggs, however, I
wondered why I was resisting. I decided instead to appoint one of our
Romanesco plants to the devotion of the butterfly. Let them have it.
Of course. We had read *The Hungry Caterpillar*. We knew how
ravenous they were. We found small twigs and, using a gentle system,
lifted up every mini beast and placed them into a small sanctuary
(created for them.
                                     We noticed some caterpillars had
different markings. Differing butterfly species – the possibility
there to precipitate the expansion of the species
as a whole. We added more leaves from our food too, but only
gave what we were happy to. *Ya Sha'afi. Ya Ka'afi*: the
Sufi esoteric principle of not too much, not too little; the required.

The next morning, a skeletal plant remained. The creamy, soft
green interlinking leaf-skin transmuted into butterfly energy on
the rise. They had triumphed. In just one night, being gifted
support in their growth from an unexpected, outside source,
their metamorphosis accelerated.
The moment we decided to allow them to *be*, rather than impeding
the perpetuation of their species, that moment we changed the
course of some kind of fate.
I gave them more leaf.
This morning: bulging, soft green changed to a proud texture.
Spiky. Patterns. Skeleton leaves. Smaller caterpillars carousing.

One, relaxed – sleeping on the outer rim of the plant pot. The vibe was good. Real good.

I await the butterfly. Our small intervention has created an inter-linking causal effect. When her wings, freshly woven from the spell, peek out, the movement shall begin. She will flutter & all of their wings will flutter. And somewhere, in space, in time, other things too shall be activated. A shifting of energy. A causal node. And when the waves of change emanating from that node reach us (& they will) we will know magic is not a choice.

It is only to be wielded & we can always participate.

)

Eve Esfandiari-Denney
—
Solo to bird phoenix
   after Farīd al-Dīn ʿAṭṭār

     I know you can see through my body,
its soft little bones
its heart-shrill rhythm.
I forget how astral everything is, that my suffering

is equivocal to my orchard, the number of orange fruits that exist.

     I love the way your beak is pierced with exactly a thousand holes.
     Each opening has a different sound, each sound is a secret.

Phoenix, I tried to rip the skin off a snake instead of letting it moult.
I tried to block sunlight with my body, save a fly from a swimming pool.

(I've tried to live my life in one breath,
tried rebirth, trusted I am a butterfly
dreaming as a woman; the fact there are realised beings.

Don't tell Oaba, Baba-joon
about my drinking
rainwater through dirt.

About my opening the door to death like a boathouse.
That I am only blood mixed with dust and dust
and the world might persuade you otherwise.

what vultures are singing

Hello,   will you cry your heart out
when I address you;   Commissioner Seahorse, Delegate Butter
Angel   Speaker Warm Water
Council of all gentle things.

I am seventeen and dying of cancer   today
someone read my body back. Its blood type,   the atomic weight
the   number   of   bones;   I don't trust any of them
so contingent   on each other,   on gentle things.

Council, it hurts when you   lead me in by   my carpet burns,
by my ankles.   Even during   slow moving
traffic,   this fruit drink   you could let me
leave. I imagine I can go anywhere   to fibre-optic cables
or submarine cables   at any moment I could cross
the Atlantic. I am already leaving moving like   landscapes   do

)

so elastic, like   how there is   a place to tread
between   hell and   the light from the fridge or,
how there are so many sim cards beneath the Ozone.   They are
hidden everywhere, the same as ants.   To you,

I hold up one big hand   then one little hand   as if surrender
can be had.   I'm asking you   Agent
Milkweed,   understudy to   Seahorse,
formerly known as   Rain Bird,   all gentle.

Would you   make me   fight   there is more
to life than more   of it. To conserve is   to imagine
permanence as if   we could not revert back to what we were
before,   we could not
be proteins. Let me   trade

Eve Esfandiari-Denney

a light for my home   when my powered down body   is entire   in the bath   after dinner, it's tired it can't keep tiring.   You know the reason a bird sings in the morning is to confirm she survived the night you know to survive   is to gather what you have until something changes   my alkalines,   my blindfold beyond medicine, the familiar lilt in a voice moving closer; all   gentle things   turn
around.   I had you I'll undo myself to see you again again   please everything again.

(

After Leyly

O my ovarian health! the beat of ah! the white of your eyes,
the white of your eyes so like glass-bottled milk your mouth
so mouth i do drunken love i do i do lay down my lights
beside a plate of tomatoes

you grated *thank you*; i want to laugh like you now,
prove to everyone that has loved you they were right
every night-walking Juliette every girl Saint
Flora clean from the body

they will hold you up one by one with one
hundred found strong arms like we all should have. Please wait,
let me store your breaths in sound fields so i can play them back,
then play them again in reverse until morning, morning lay down
your lights like a sun controlling a world again what a well

choreographed thing you you bending the tendons
of my knees so my thighs are against my chest are against   )
my ah's my every my every bright bone will
break   by tenderness   here is a party made out of almost no one.

Just rice and string, the smell of your room, your body in shorts,
a big goose in my chest
          my goose my goose my goose my goose

will you find a way to get into the ground so you can hear
a ring sound glowing; lean too far forward into its heat
straining to say and then saying *i do*

*not hope for a fresh water fountain; a new white saint bird;
a deep down down animal.* i don't want any of it i don't
want the name someone else will give me.

She will call me water but i will be moving an ore
an ore in water Leyly Leyly *there is no such thing as repetition.
Only insistence* i wake up tomorrow without you without
you there sleeping and say it again.

Jack Barker-Clark

—

Cowl

1

After the restaurant, we come upon a vole. Shorn, leering, eager, birthmarked, crimped, streaked, flat. It lies in death as if painted. Kerbside artwork in the subject's own blood and skin. There had been a furore at the table. Weather, senses, the waiter's soft sheen. But nowadays my love of militant plate-clearing can rescue even the starkest evening. Our boy waves goodnight to the vole. Its tail is so short. We leave it there, whispering in the dust.

2

Once a month I reek of varnish. Our pine furniture demands to be lacquered. It absorbs. We don't. Openly we critique at the dinner table. Forks, geopolitics. Once, I came home to flies. A dozen sluggish bluebottles ambling, butting the windowpane. We assembled the vacuum's extensions, telescopes. Each buzz extinguished as bodies rattled through the chamber. The mystifying crosswords haunted us all evening. We roasted a dozen parsnips to ash.

3

Our son is two now, almost three. In praise of routine. He cannot stop singing Christmas carols, new and old. The verbs he mashes, the choruses are amplified. He sings while I precision-wash these dishes. I dunk them to the sound of trilling crescendos as the light streams in. I have started blunting every twinkling knife, pre-empting an event that will never happen. I am obsessed with the thought that one day our boy will stab me through the heart.

4

The menus are glossy, sun-faded images. We see vegan fish and chips, some kind of long runner bean, seaweed. Strong, thick, demonstrative chips. My father-in-law sits in silence until the food arrives, at which point he launches into a tirade on snowflakes, on pansies. He is fresh from his lifeless BMW and doesn't stay. The hairy hand dismissing us through the window floats wretched in isolation, a ghost trying to shake off its own skin.

5
Every weekend, I go after myself, dredge up the compact dictionary, memorise words I ought to know. Profligacy (the depraved), insuperable (these afternoons). I labour in the shrapnel-strewn kitchen. The radio's grubby inflorescence. Our fulsome hosts. Once I singed my hair on a Bunsen burner and every now and again all I can smell is sadness.

6
The boulders in our valley are so improvident. They tumble and freeze. Narrow air scoops millstone from the block. I ramble, scurry, sit. Alternate which leg drapes over the other, my dry-cleaned trousers, their corporate patina. I wait for nothing to happen, but a train always bursts through the hillside. The clouds are alive, unshakeable. They have dreamt up their billion formulas and manufacture them endlessly in light.

)

7
Soon a fog arrives. Cloying, it outstrips the lacquer. Through our window it drifts and I cannot sleep. There are sheep in the fields in our valley, daubed in blue, in red. I think of them as I thrash. They winter together but never huddle. At the top of the vale I encounter them at their drinking trough. One of them has newly died, its body enlarged, a raincloud in shifting wind. It has always been my ambition to run a stream, a brook, through this garden, but I am becoming despondent in the extreme around water.

8
Once, too old, too wise for curfews, I sat my parents down – solemnly, in wicker chairs, ready to sack them. Nobody else was held to the clock, for it was not conducive to being a serious person, not *de rigueur*. I collected pound coins and silver from my grandparents, a sort of work-experience archaeologist. Took my haul out to the youth club. It was unclear which boy first glassed the other, but the blood from their heads crept out like shame.

9

I send videos to my parents, as if we are in hiding, exile. Snippets of our boy in song. Through albums, jigsaws, the miniature life, I scroll. But all I see are kerbsides, smears, the vole we'd witnessed scrawled up its banking. When I ask myself who took these pictures, I refuse to understand. Later that evening, already they are gone. No tyre-flattened creatures, tarmac, stone. In vain I shuffle these jpegs. I pace all night in my suspicion.

10

Asleep, I am lowered into warm water. Not a swimming pool, an eddy. Drowning patterns at the savage indoor silo. I jolt as the evening pulls me down, cowering at my imagination. I awake to a shuffling. Indiscriminate animals dining in our narrow flue. They rub against brick, a code, a warning. They scratch out their messages. They bury themselves alive.

11

There is a lake in our village, its water like metal. As kids, we forged through its reeds. I remember empty bags, a crowbar. Such a pale night. The water dividing under my tensile movements. Dwarf pine, fog. Up ahead a pretty boathouse, twinkling sienna. I writhed in my new understanding, catastrophe coming. To survive it I disappeared. Bright galleries, carnivals. I tell this story to my son. He asks what happened at the boathouse. I don't remember. I have never gone back there.

12

Now everything is lacquered, this house of pine. I am turning into one of these dining chairs. Caustic, waiting to bruise. What's the phrase? *Too much pine / though sublime / makes the brain / . . .* something. At nursery, my boy draws impressionistic faces. Sinks them in whirlpools. We are invited in for discussion. Soft play, shrunken chairs. The new marketplace for terror. *Has there been any death in the family?*

13

We travel north, wade in rockpools. No muscles, seaweed, crabs. Just cuttlefish running errands – window-shopping on their lunchbreak. Away we come with rashes, atoll-shaped, rings on our calves. I collect the antibiotics, twelve caplets in a braille-pocked box. We criticise ourselves as we swallow them. For doing it wrong, the swallowing. Too decorous. Our contribution to antimicrobial resistance. Our calling it a night.

14
The fridge sags with oil paintings. It swarms but our walls are so bare. Stripped but for two well-worn oars, mounted crosswise on the old chimneybreast. Scarred faces. The kind that turn over so sadly. Not once have either of us heard the other express their love of rowing. I see trimmed waves, shortening under my paddle, but refuse to remember the detail. We eat up our broccoli and tackle the evening's anagrams. In the morning we are so scrambled we forget to war.

15
On the coast, amusement parks shine with seafoam. Walls, towers, trebuchets of water. A puppet reads our fortune. The card prints out. *You will only ever be disappointed*, it doesn't quite say. Inside slot-machines live llamas. Trapped jackals, cheetahs, cats. The smoking ban has long come into effect but dank curtains of air tumble like cloth. On the cliffside bend, the car breaks down. Something about gaskets. Fluid. We limp to the burger van and order our hot dogs. The vender runs out of onions. His regulars berate him from the dirt.

16
On Tuesday I traipse in the fields, a dozen smiling ramblers. So many elms have surrendered here. Out-wintered larch. It is the morning of the wedding, or is it the funeral, in the valley where I was born. I have raked all my leaves and buttered all my crackers. Today someone will move into an urn and we will praise him for all eternity. I have sent the deceased a tarot card but no longer remember what for. Everyone here has their poppy on. Everyone here has a hateful little speech.

17
At night I cannot sleep. I rise and scramble through the dark. Wretched in the underpass, wind ghosting on the fields. I visit the kerbside by the restaurant. Stones so clean, intact. No vole, no smear, no violence. In

the midnight window, the chairs sit like squatters. The free bar at the wake had moved us all into hatred. With a lecture I put myself to bed. In the morning, I will ask my boy if he remembers a death in the valley. I will ask my boy if he remembers who has died.

18
There is another bird in our chimneybreast, scrambling in the masonry. A cowl fitter has come. Deftly, he untangles his ladder, a gangly, unappeasable insect. We hear him on the slate, a premium clambering. In our valley there is such a thing as rejuvenation. We take pride in our roofs, our guttering, our gargoyles. We perch in the living room. We count out our banknotes. We seal all our skeletons in.

(

Emily Cooper & Jo Burns

—

from *The Conversation*

M.T.W

Sketch of a mistress

Dora, it's not easy to be wrenched away.
I wonder if you happily cultivated

your image, as a renowned
stealer of rings, your shiny conquests.

Did you relish the scandal?
I'm no judge, I hardly did any different

so what is it that gives the impression   )
that you aren't averse to side-shows

or even the label homewrecker?
I became accustomed to that insult once,

from Olga. I learnt that three are a tiding,
a charm, a gulp. I weighed whens not whys

in my beak and for a while became expert
in the dark arts. I learnt to mimic the ways

of a thief, his tricks-in-flight, his evening habits.
And I wonder if on overcast nights,

your nape also plumes, aching for dawn,
or your scapulars for an honest man.

Having been wrenched away, to be reflected
by stolen treasures, painted as someone you're not

is to understand you were only a decoy,
to the fickle, from the very start.

Sometimes I imagine you scavenging
illusions of grandeur, fed lie by lie

to keep you in his wicker cage until
you find that glimmer has no bones to pick on.

(

D.M

Double Exposure

Marie-Thérèse,

It is important to face yourself face on
Do not shy away from your own reflection

Perhaps if you took the time to wrestle
With yourself. Heels of your palms hard

Against the splintered wood of the studio floor
Scraping up the monochrome oils

With your pointing finger. Because each
Of your fingers is a pointing finger when

You make a fist. Contrast yourself   )
Against yourself. Paint the background first

Allow the image to reveal itself. You don't
Have to try quite so hard. Capture it

The moment it has happened. Too late
Development is inevitable in this light

M.T.W

Fist-fight in front of Guernica

Dora, what hurt me was not your fists
or even him in your clutch.

It was his passivity as we hissed
at each other. He'd told me before

about Guernica; how it was for me,
the extent of his love. I'd accepted his use

of my blood but still...
A woman knows when something is up.

The one in his new work was elegant, sharp,
sleek and dark. And here you were, claiming

it all. I asked him *Pablo, which one of us leaves?*
and he weighed me, gentle, against you, smart.

Dora, you know he refused to decide;
not truly yours but no longer mine.

We grappled, writhed. But what's a few bruises
compared to being drawn as you die slowly?

More painful than those new sketches of me;
increasingly ugly, pastelled and blurred,

was my victimhood, portrayed by him
contrasted with glamour and monochrome.

And then the smirk as we both bled;
The choicest experience of my life, he said.

Dora, can you imagine yet how it feels
to see through art how undesired you are?

D.M

A Ring with a Spike Inside

On balance there was and is no harmony
Things observed are never owned

The light that touched the canvas
Left again, there are no scuff marks

On the floor
I cleaned my nails of you

We were collected
You and I

Projected onto white emulsion walls
It is a job in itself shaking loose

)

I consider writing you a letter
Instead I send him a rusty spade

I have furrowed deep enough inside
Your head, I will always be the other

M.T.W

Girl Before a Mirror

Yes, you'll always be *la otra*. Me?
Under etiquette, I want to be fury.

He kept me so busy within myself,
that I burnt alive at both your edges.

I became a ghost and turned insane
then he palmed me off to his friend Lacan.

When you arrived, it sucked air
from my cheeks, as I fell into nebulae

which I still dread will burst me.
Helping him aspire to be bigger than stars,

(

I swallowed years, ripped open scars
but today I found a poem in all the strife.

It asked When did you hand him your life?

D.M

An Analysis

In the terracotta bathroom of my new apartment
With its bath that leans against the wall

I look in the mirror above the sink
And see Lacan looking back

I memorise the lines we
Drew out together on the table

He declined to use his office
Instead had his student drive me

To a restaurant for our appointment
That boy out there, he pays me for the privilege

)

We discuss you, and him, and him, and him
Again. I want to talk about you, my reflection

But we end up back at the mirror. By dessert
He has stopped asking questions, instead

He tells me about his art. About techniques
I might want to know about, his idea

For a three-dimensional paint, with aspirations
For the fourth as well. It's time for me to leave

I decline his invitation for a brandy up the stairs
Sometimes a cigar is not just a cigar

This six-poem sequence is part of a collaborative project in which Dora Maar (D.M.) and Marie-Thérèse Walter (M.T.W.), who were both lovers of Picasso, are corresponding.

Alan Fielden

—

from *Container*

Take your hands off me.
Put your hand on my shoulder.
Hold my face in your hands.
He put his hands around her throat like this.
She put her hand on the knife like this.
She kisses his hands like this.
She puts her hand around his throat like this.
He puts his hand on the handle of the knife like this.
He kisses her open hands like this.
She puts her hand around the blade of the knife like this.
They press their bodies together like this.
They press their bodies together in the bed like this.
They press their bodies together in the rain, like this.
They press their bodies together in the back of the lorry like this.
(They are pressed together on the screen like this.
They are found, pressed together, in the back of the lorry like this.
They are buried, pressed together, in the ground, like this.
They are together like this.
They are found, pressed together, in the ground, like this.
They are found like this.
They are buried kissing.
They are found kissing.
They are kissing in the ground.
She is found with her hands around his throat.
They press their hands together.
They press their throats together.
They have melted together, like this.
They find their hands together.
Their hands are buried in the ground, together.
They kiss the ground together.
They are found kissing each other's throats, together.
They are ground down, together.
They are buried in their mouths together.

They bury their hands together.
They are discovered, together.
They are found dead together.
They have turned to liquid together.
They say goodnight darling with their hands, like this.
They say I love you with their hands, like this.
They say sleep well honey with their hands like this.
They pray with their hands, together, like this.
He says I miss you, with his hands, like this
She says I want you, with her hands, like this.
They say goodbye, with their hands, like this.
They wave goodbye, with their hands, at the same time, like this.
They wave goodbye, at the same time.
At the same time, they go, like this.
Like this, they go.
At the same time, like this.

)

ajw
—
Sink In / III

(

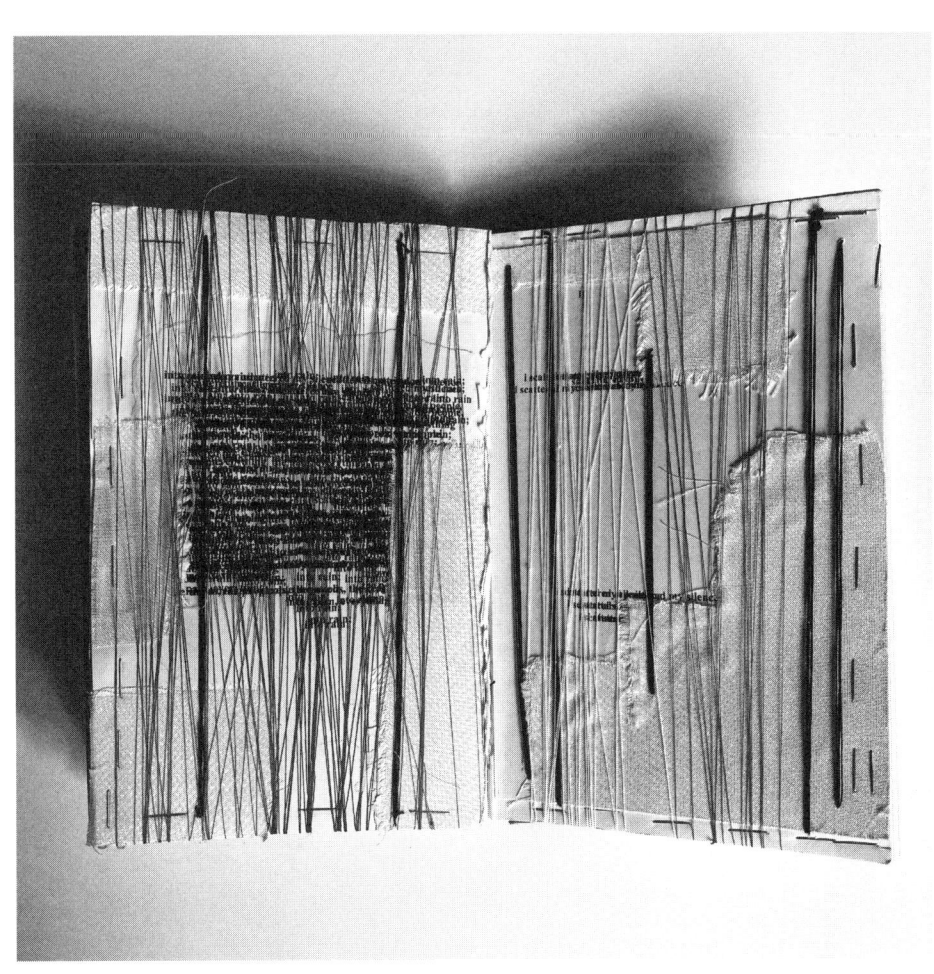

ajw

(

'Sink In / III' is from a larger constellation of works ranging from video installation and photography to poetry, that takes Hito Steyerl's essay 'Missing People: Entanglement, Superposition and Exhumation as Sites of Indeterminacy' as a reference point for examining blurry and indeterminate images as a means to open up personal trauma and PTSD. Overtly hidden and embedded within itself, the work remains as secretive as the trauma it expresses, allowing for a public expression of grief that remains private through its resistance to becoming public.

Laura Elliott

—

Sprawl Song

Picked a poster
with the shapes on
   they are definitely
breasts   five blue
breasts in a row

where am I going
to hang all
these breasts!
   Sympathetic
mound study

I am light-headed
   front-loaded
   taking care of
hardnesses
   rubbing lotions

(

into the surface
of the skin
   the cracked heels
and the stretched
stomach

accommodating
as it has always been
   Louise Bourgeois
watching my headrush
building steadily

from where I've
propped her portrait
on the embroidered
sofa cushions
   posed

in her bulbous
suit encrusted with
whatever that is
   a wattle and daub
raspberry

maybe
   above her tiny
brown shoes and
amused face
out in the street

   it must be Manhattan   )
with all those
stoops and that
particular shade
of autumn grief.

   Look at these geologic
cobs on my shoulders
   she is saying
   potatoes are a
cumulative landscape

   and anyway
when did you last
speak to your mother!
   Louise I'm sorry
to do this to you

Laura Elliott

    what was meant to be
a closer more tender
observation
    has turned into
a distracted excorporation

    matching your
plaster gut suit
with my very own
protuberance
    and loving how

now Louise
    you and I both appear
to be leaking
breasts all over
my apartment

(swelling and melting
off our chests
like candle wax
    an extra lobe
popping out

as my belly button
uncouples itself
beneath the elasticated
waistband
    soft as a kiss!

Let loose all over
our breasts roam
the walls
    like the snails
decimating the allotment

   free to do
whatever they want
amidst the sprawling
wormwood
   hung

like half-chewed
toffees from
the underside
of the chamomile stems
in the heat.

Observe the breasts
explode!
   There they go again
by the nursery
   all the toddlers setting fire

to the forest school   )
   as I toss snail shells
one by one
into the blackberry bushes
like sick nuts

   as fistfuls of gooseberries
flinch in my bra.
   It is the month
of the mouth
of the snail I decide

   one glued to the bricks
like a stud
I want to kick open
   just to see
what's inside

Laura Elliott

    one crawling
through the window
during the night
    as Louise half-watches
over me and the baby

    snails on the pillowcase
sugar on my tongue
    my house becoming
a garden and
my body

becoming a house
    where there is
a turquoise rise
on the Turkish rug
    it is me again Louise

(arching my torso
like you taught me!
    I am a whole
room dedicated
to something inflating

    our breasts fully loaded
again dangling
from the ceiling
like nylon mesh stockings
stuffed full of sand

    a corona of nipples
rippling the rim
of my fireplace
    dogs barking at the men
as they each stand up

whenever our breasts
enter the conversation
   pendulous and
damp to
the touch.

   I've never been so
medically accounted for
   nor so sober
in my new lumpen
woman costume

   so many interventions
in this flat routine
   peeling the beetroot
   carving the bread batons
   rubbing and rolling

the flesh like masa   )
   trying to feel
the baby pulse
in the hollow
of my palms.

   There are so
many ways it can all
go wrong Louise
   but as long as
you're still watching

I'll keep trying
   I turn each of your
shapes to mine
   the herbal suit dilates
as grass flushes

the edges of the plot
and little mushroom
children sprout
up all over us!
    It is truly growing season

    here try on a
silk shirt the size
of a small cow
    yes that will look great
as I squat among

the leaves   a crotchless
    shapeless gape
    spurred on
by the movement
of plants

(our breasts like
ropes of ivy
plotting
a direct route
to the sun

    you should see
the aerial roots
bend horizontal
across the living
room!

    Love is a channel
running despite us
Louise with our
soap-rind labour and
oat pressure-headaches

— Laura Elliott

our bucking midriffs
and wild breasts
garlanded into
the parched grass
of our diaries

   there is still plenty
of time left
   I keep telling you
Louise still plenty
of costumes to go.

)

Chrissy Williams

–

Congruence

≅

the door opens and my not-boyfriend nods at his guitar

the door is behind me and the cold stone floor flexes

I forget the door and lean into the neck of my not-boyfriend

we make no music under the black stars of the ceiling

≅

someone is dead on the tarmacked tennis courts

the basset hounds investigate with great integrity

I hand out magnifying glasses to passers-by

Pistachios has run out of decaf lattes

≅

the show cannot start without a velvet curtain

the improvisers are almost all disappointed

I realise 'my type' is always an arsehole

why is the usher still handing out tickets?

≅

night-time is just a time of day here

we can all have sex whenever we want

there are a lot of people in this car park

the sun cannot be switched off with a clapper

≅

my not-boyfriend has a silver thumb ring

he looks like an impression of a teenager

conversation is difficult in a basement

I remember I have to submit my tax return

≅

I see a flock of small Italian greyhounds

working out if they already know me

they huddle in a scrum to make their decision

then scatter up into the brisk morning sky

≅

an improviser mimes folding down an ironing board

the laughter crescendos – everyone is impressed

instead of seats on stage there is just one tricycle

this sex scene is going to be complicated

≅

someone's vagina is open in front of me

I wonder what's most polite to put in it

everyone in this dark room seems happy

it turns out we didn't need any beds

)

≅

we cannot catch the murderer because it is Tuesday

and the bins all have to be collected on Wednesday

plus there is a minor obstruction on the A303

just before the first turning to Weymouth

≅

the guide dog assembly is going great

point of order, gavel, Labrador speaks:

why aren't I allowed to eat chocolate?

whose Nissan Micra was that in the forecourt?

≅

my not-boyfriend needs to come before mum arrives

I jerk him off in the living room briskly

he comes in an endless wave across the coffee table

one nosy cat gets caught in the cross-fire

≅

the improvisers want to assess our creative writing

everybody holds out videotapes

of Freddie Mercury in a yellow leather jacket

a boy cries and has a quiet epiphany

I flip over the vulva's folds like I'm reading a book

I lick a fingertip before turning the next page

I am very intrigued, academically speaking

I am uncertain about the necessity for footnotes

)

Jay Gao

—

Body Sonnet

I.

Behind us

I had a dream you returned to me in the borderlands

II.

There is no doubt remaining in our day

(

that imperial history has to be repeated every night,

III.

Re-open time like the cloche on our

       earbuds pressing themselves in

              dream-brought.

          There is the nonviolence of one into stone into

IV.

                                              did the breath of those

inert evenings feel celestial even before a thing of joy

hospital windows from the last night ever.

I wanted to end it by any natural means; one last plea for what is

    subjected.

V.

what could I do or travel to in order   )

    to order his body into a space not filled in with tradition

        a ghost ship glides in like the ending.

            I was in an enormous beyond;

                I believed in the grey water

                    in a diver,

                                a sedated rubber tyre.

VI.

                    Abecedarian work

            I fantasise what I could do

      sleep, wake, herd his opinions on religion

and things

and

VII.

(bewilder if you can.

      Like it if you could almost presage his language.

      I didn't know you would be stateless.

                    If I did

            I would have ceased from

VIII.

these nations

found he himself had changed history.

      he was a beggar back in the real world

            he, who never conquered what

IX.

      Oh!

Zealot There is nothing free of bass still asleep,   )

he found he had transformed into

X.

Hero,

what were you at the time;

      setting fire to the larger picture;

      setting fire to the protest on the surface;

      settling   down

XI.

one sleep slipped into the centre

of the air, through his Chinese doors, like a bouquet

                                        banquet

XII.

Last night over our valley a version of me never became domesticated.

I fled to flee from another sweet trap,

(an oil

XIII.

I wonder if you covet. The weight of my soul

faded from a foreign guest, never preventing the epic

XIV.

My heart

The sand,

the blood

in

the water?

Should be

an illusion

)

Martha Kapos

—

Impromptu

> *...music must vanish in the act of being made*
> *– Lawrence Kramer*

A glossy black piano standing in a room.

A patient small agony. Pressed together

the thin keys lie still with their lips closed.

They huddle in a long white line of boats high in the water

— doldrum notes on the lookout for any possible wind:

(the weather hovering in each key.

                                              In a sudden act of coming alive

she lies down in my head to be the breath from the four corners.

There's a thought inside each finger disturbing the keys

as if they were lips about to part.

The small dimensions of my hand shoot out

to slip a note under a closed door.

                                              It is picked up by the wind.

Between movement and breath

one by one the notes dance cheek-to-cheek, touching

and losing touch down the wistful white horizontal –

                                        in the sudden act of coming alive

she had laid down in my head.   But the words are goodbye.

There is nothing left – the moment it is about to be.

Floating above a feeling of defeat, a boat must go out

in order to come back.

It enters the harbour flying unknown colours.

)

Instrument

At first it belonged
to the long realm of the stare
at arm's length from my eye

a glossy black piano
standing nervously in a room.

*

Looking at it, I understood
an I and a you: the you

a great looming box
appeared to be asleep

as if the silent white surface of a face
tucked into a large bed

could hold a lively four-sided world
in deep hiding out of sight.

*

A black lid had closed all of it away
inside a very near longing.

I approached and sat down
in front of you
and stretched out my ten thousand fingers.

Xuela Zhang

—

Quarantine I

In this real, rolling, crisis
of justifiable abstractions,

loneliness overlapped
without violence.

The daylight,
as usual, faithful.

Occasionally a wind
refines a way of self-

possession. On our walks, the air,
separating the trees, and the animals,

)

separating the grass with the rush
of small entireties,

say *listen,*
       you need not have noticed.

I think about the things
I need not have noticed—

our tidal over- and under-
estimations.

Quarantine II

The sea had a way of turning—
it made recoiling
a slow and constant sensation.

The entire shore breathed
regardless of tension,
an endless version of the pelvis—

she said you could not see
this muscle, but it would move.
Imagine this part of you

sucking up a piece of tissue.
Very counter-intuitive, she added.
You caught yourself breathing carefully

but completely wrongly.
He insisted on talking; you looked
up, and became absorbed

in the pink, rubbed clouds.
Elsewhere, it was experienced
as 'the tornado'. *Was it unbelievable*

to see one house destroyed,
and the one next to it
untouched, asked the anchor.

Yeah, unbelievable.

Translator's Note III

Last winter, you watched the members of your family—
that is, the three of you—settle in their own ways
in an emergency room.

You felt a loss in this kind of knowledge about family,
as if you had started to fear that all of you
might lose your ability to comment on each other.

If god exists,
he must be in the ceiling light of
every hospital—

the body was a given thing;
its clarity is now convincing
beyond control.

*   )

My father looked at the floor
silently, up to a point.

My mother and I kept asking
the questions we thought
were worth asking.

Humanity is eventually different
from being human—

humanity is a faith
in all the unnatural efforts
you made.

Scott Thurston

—

from *FAILSAFE*

*

for Andrew Holmes

Took out but could not get back our relation to above. Allow yourself to be lifted in the morning session of immanence – can we combine the two? But at the same time alive. Buzzard over verge. Heat of presence bound to the quality of no longer ours to be owned. Stalk unattached presence – what do you turn to, to be here?

IS THE WITNESS DANCING?

(yesterday the view
too vulnerable for you
consciously span the bridge
we dive through the centre
the still weekend
occupy that quality

don't get attached, witness
space around and within
where do they coincide?

lie on the floor
not aiming for lightning
but something more

*

All of it given space – hold everything on a line in time, gathered-in. They bring gifts to synthesise and complete: from, in, within; to and from the physical centre. Quiet simple courage moving forward and back towards resolution and unfolding – allow it to be given space.

*

Most last for no reason, the torso in front of my actual torso: expanded, elevated, made up of hot energy, full and implacable. Not everything makes desired content. Fill it with information? Earth makes me cry in chaos. To give an account, transition of loss.

*

Failsafe. Would you seek it if you lost it, realise the secret? Different pitch, rate of change, the birds out of the tree. Things at least related. We do not stop. To not think ahead. Are we together as, or together with? Who knows when you might move your hand down, blind to motion. Body shapes the heart. I am earth moving.

)

*

Trusting sub-con to enter an object, a room, material of all kinds of orders. By the end of your dance the wave calmed down. The voice of the table – from lying to crawling – let's make it move. He does not respond. Let it elevate me: to be still, an unforgivable vulnerability.

*

Do I have the right body for this? A few folk known by sight: to be witnessed, to go high energy. Accepted as and where I was. Great Salt Lake: a little lustful distraction left over later with a little guilt, a book folded in tissue. Go back to still departs, before you already.

*

With the unbroken circle the globe, leave appearances. Actually making, how detailed, how pure? I was of others, leading from my legs, had rejected earlier, articulated a kind, I accept. I accept lust. I do not accept death. I accept this difficulty with living. I do not accept this fear. I accept this fear.

*

for Bill T Jones

Adapted to living with. Perceived as contained. Might be a garden. These forms lose time, visiting them, noticing how they. Creature of the body, arduous and crazy. Show internal landscape. Don't think something as experience in language. In world setting up obstacle, ambush, sabotage. To have to be in the body in a violent relationship to the world.

(Thinking is stopping. Where you become who you. Never stops. Who can think are acting. Every day has to stop, clear. This is what fire looks like. Are they past watching clouds? And who are you to do that? Your responsibility is to create a common.

*

for Maggie O'Sullivan

Secure history enabled. Noting, or rather asking at one point, can I dance you my thoughts? I know this bird because I heard it in your poem. Showing respect to yourself. Remember it always. Extend time to make a different choice. Give the cry into low sun. Pick up a small white feather, true as the world.

Anticipating remembering. Giving me strength. Lapwings in the book the colour of my car. What make it was. Summertime sadness revenge night-time procrastination. Now resuming in the present – here she comes, there is time. A history of shadows.

*

Difficult hill – who sees only through climbing. When otherwise in me break. Oh knees. Coming down the hill in animal – breaking the tail-light. Not too thick nor too fleet. Are we naming or framing? How to loosen the double-pattern, the pleasure arising? Don't fully grasp it. Could come up with a solid hand rail between the senses and the spirit.

*

To cry, to stay as long as that writerly dance throws, jumps, turns, hops and stops at the end of the phrase. I remember paradise. Tools of reception, projection, carving the space. Strength of words, phrase upon phrase, accompanying the line leading up to the eye. The eye is lost by us at the end of the phrase.

)

Rory Cook

—

Of Imitation

I observed a distinct stooping, which hardens,

awkwardly, as memory. Yet no luck — the shimmer's

temporary, the gesture's permanent. Swift, sheer

grace repeats in childish light: surfaces newly spoken of

flaunt their slippery backwash. Those untraceable,

hurried exposures… seized-upon patterns… though

already I loved you. Clean tones echo from lonely

(hands clapping in detail, rubber tips on chair legs,

an elegance is haunting. This sentence, followed by a pause.

Useless Setting

in which to find the reality,
the sure heart of scale. Then they
decline, retreat; absence
approaches. The night does not
achieve the night.

Would you appreciate
a spirit of hopelessness, dim
bearings at the rough edge?
Overdetermined trees exaggerate
on the limb. Oil clings

to skin like splendour,
panic and sleep.

)

Ralf Webb

—

Dark Wood

Each time you say that you hate someone, a scar appears across your heart. Adam said that to me once. He's getting married soon, and his partner's expecting. I couldn't have guessed he'd have a baby at this age. I always saw him as old and haggard, fathering a child at fifty, fat with beer and sadness. But people surprise you.

His mum, Grace, came by Texaco a few weeks ago when I was working. She told me all about it. I'd just started there after a long period without a job. It wasn't appropriate for her to chuck all this information at me at work. I'd go as far as to say she shouldn't've even said hello, because it completely threw my concentration, and I probably seemed incompetent. When she told me about Adam, I felt as if dark water was rushing through my insides very quickly. I smiled. Eventually I said to Grace, 'That's very nice, I'm happy.'

'It's been so long, come and visit us at the house,' she said. Adam and his fiancée were living with her temporarily, she went on, to wait for the baby.

I sold her the petrol and twenty Lamberts.

'Can't get the monkey off my back,' Grace said, and tapped the cigarettes with two of her pudgy yellowed fingers.

She got in her car and left.

Adam would argue that my heart's covered in scars, because I used to hold a lot of hate. But I don't think negatively like that anymore. I'm older now. I think positively. This morning, for example, I wake up early, drink herbal tea and eat eggs.

Protein's good brainfood. Then I sit still and concentrate on a feeling of warmth. A doctor told me about it once. It's a technique of sorts, to manifest positive outcomes in your life. I imagine there's a ball of white light behind my sternum, glowing.

Grace lives in a bungalow called Sunrise Cottage. It's in a cul-de-sac behind the woods. At the fag-end of the arse-end of town, is what Adam'd say. I used to spend a lot of time there. Me and him were very close in that way. But we had an altercation about money, which I've come to learn is how all altercations start, more or less. We fell out of touch. I didn't even realise I missed him, until Grace came by the petrol station.

I've thought about it a lot since she asked me, and today feels right. I think: *I'm coming, I'm coming to knock on your door.* I project this thought into the universe as powerfully as I can. I want for Adam to grasp it in his soul and to share in my feeling of warmth and excitement, and Grace too. And Adam's partner, even though I don't know her yet. So I set out for Sunrise Cottage.

Town's dead. A Sunday in the middle of August. Pools of light, dried leaves in dried puddles, broken and butt-filled glasses outside The Oak. And all the closed shutters in the boring precinct. Dan Harris's dad is slumped on the curb by Hong Kong House, with a can of Special Brew.

'Good day for it,' he says.

'Yeah,' I say.

'Where you going then?'

'Dark Wood.'

'Spelunking?'

'Nah.'

His legs are crossed. His ankles look like waterlogged meat, crammed into those tattered leather loafers. I used to feel sad for Mr Harris. But maybe that's presumptive. He might be happy with his life. After all, everyone in town knows him by sight and by name.

At the edge of town I follow the footpath by Hawthorne Manor, then cross the field. I think about Adam's seventeenth birthday, when we trespassed on Hawthorne Estate. I like to pass the time this way, remembering things. I like to settle on a scene, and try very hard to hover above it, like a drone. Because I don't want to see the past solely from my perspective. Most people create memories as if they're building a house to live in and furnish to their liking. The memories have to be just so, just to their private tastes and specifications. Well it shouldn't be like that. Memories should be like a big church or municipal hall filled with people, and everyone's sitting in a circle and letting each other speak and tell their own version of events. That way, you can really learn something about yourself and the world.

On Adam's seventeenth birthday we had a picnic on the Estate, down by the river. Just me, him and his girlfriend at the time. Midges hovered headache-like over the brown water. We were drinking beer and at some point I had to pee, so I went behind a bush. When I came back, Adam and his girlfriend were kissing. Adam even had his hand on her knee. In fact, he was poking a finger through a penny-size hole in her tights, and wiggling it back and forth. His mouth was red like a strawberry. I remember being angry. I felt they'd acted unfairly in some way. But I wonder if Adam remembers it the same, and what *he* felt. For example, he might've thought I was a pervert or Peeping Tom, because I stood there and watched.

I reach the bottom of the field. There's a door-shaped hole in the hedgerow. I step through and climb a slope up to the railway line, taking the shortcut into Dark Wood. Thirty metres or so on the left, the tracks hug a hillside, creating a blind bend. We used to play chicken here. No one ever got hurt. Though Dan Harris claimed he got within an inch of a train one time.

I look up and down the tracks.

There's a deer. Right beside the rails, next to the bend.

It's a buck. Curled up.

And it's dead. I can tell that almost instantly. It has a certain look, like something's been sucked out of it.

The deer's enormous. The biggest I've ever seen, I think.

An image appears in my mind: flashes of metal and red, three carriages cutting right through that buck and spraying its insides everywhere. But it doesn't look like it's been hit by a train. All its pieces are together. There's no splatter on it, or the tracks.

I climb the track fence; several taut silver wires that look like an empty music sheet. *Twang*. That vibration will probably shoot all the way along the valley, maybe all the way to the coast. I tread across the sleepers one by one. The timber feels gummy underfoot. It discharges a damp smell that recalls rot. Rotting chicken coops in Grace's garden. Rotting fruit, food waste in the dumpsters behind Texaco.

Another image: the deer leaping to life and knocking me unconscious on the tracks, so that I'm the one that gets cut-up by a train.

The dull silver rails gleam in a flash of sunlight. The deer's coat is rust-gold, rust-red, broken embers in a bonfire. My hand hovers above its back, then I touch it. There's some warmth to it, but it's a shallow warmth. From the sun, likely.

I step over the deer's body and crouch by its face.

I don't think I've been so close to an animal's face before, except Grace's dogs, may they rest in peace.

The antlers are pearled with thumb-sized half-globes and ridges. One of the eyes is missing. The empty socket is a pink-grey colour, swollen and puckered.

A gust blows through the trees on the other side of the tracks. The branches go *rush rush rush*. I could've said to Adam, *Why don't you two get a room?* and made a joke out of it. But I just stood, and watched. Finger-hole-strawberry-mouth.

I grab the deer's antlers and stretch it out. I crouch and lift the forelegs over my shoulder, gripping one in each hand, and squat to test its weight. I stand, so that it's carried on my back, and feel the lean torso conform to my posture. I'm stronger physically now than I've ever been before. It's what happens when you eat good brainfood and work hard and manifest positive outcomes.

There's a fishy smell. Black gunk leaks from the deer's backside, over the backs of my trousers. *Excessively abject.* That scrap of a phrase is cast off from some wheel in my memory. I overheard somebody, a stranger, say it once about Mr Harris, walking past Mr Harris as he snored-off a cider binge in the precinct.

I wait for a while on the tracks. Ten, fifteen seconds. Half a minute. I try to think if the first trains've come and gone yet. There's one an hour going east, one going west. Lumbering two-carriage trains that seem ten years past decommission. The heft of me and the deer combined would be enough to derail one, probably. And what would the driver say? How would they explain it?

I pivot over the fence on the opposite side of the tracks, manoeuvring the deer with me, and slide down the verge through bindweed, brambles, tattered plastic bags and drinks cans.

I reach the edge of Dark Wood and lay the deer down on the earth. The bright tree leaves, like a colander, let the light pour down in columns. I sit and smell the dirt and the scent of deer muck.

Then there's a rapid twanging in the fence wires, and a horn-blare from the eastbound train as it thunders round the corner and surges past me and the deer, sucking and shouting at the air, frightening birds from bushes and stoking such a scare in me I suddenly need to piss.

Dan Harris a big fat liar. If he'd come within an inch of a train he'd be dead.

A stillness comes over the woods again, but the westbound will follow any minute now. The deer's one eyelid has loosened open. I stand above its body and take some photos of it on my phone, avoiding that black dead eye. I take photos of its antlers, getting all those pearls and ridges into focus. I switch to the front camera and take a photo of my face. But it looks lopsided and asymmetrical, which it doesn't ordinarily look like at all, so I delete it.

I'll show Adam these photos. He likes animals. He has a huge tattoo of a grouse on his right forearm, which he got after his dad died. His dad was big into pheasant shooting, so the tattoo was in homage. But it wasn't some original idea. Everybody's parents die from cancer round here and everyone gets tattoos in homage. For example I have a black lion's head on my shoulder, because my mum was a Leo.

I was with Adam when he got his done. We went to Sunrise Cottage straight after, to borrow pub-money, or return the car to Grace, or something. His arm was still in clingfilm, plasma leaking from the edges. Grace saw the tattoo.

'If he was still alive, he'd scour it off!' she yelled.

'He'd be proud,' Adam yelled back, 'he'd be happy!'

I recall walking right between the two of them and out into the garden. I hate that poisonous talk. When someone says what somebody else *would've* done, or what somebody else *would've* thought, when it's really just what they think, and the somebody they're using to prop up their own opinion can't even speak for themselves because they're dead. There's no argument like a dead person.

I stayed put in the garden, with the dogs, and heard Adam shout the word *hate hate hate* over and over. *I hate you, I hate this house, I hate my life.* There was a ball and string attached to the rotary washer on the lawn. I remember spinning it around and watching Grace's dogs pounce and bite at the air.

I've a compulsion to find the deer a proper resting place. I don't want to leave it here for all the passengers on the trains to gawp at, like it's something in a museum.

The deer's getting stiff now, and it's even more awkward to carry. I lift it and walk through the columns of leaf-light, into the trees.

There's a tunnel system under Dark Wood that twists and coils for miles. A plaque on the public footpath shows a map of the tunnels. The map looks like those illustrations of human intestines that you see in science books, all squidgy and stacked up like paste squeezed from a tube. The tunnel system's a mix of natural caves, quarries and bunkers owned by the MOD.

I feel funny when I think too hard about all that empty space, underneath the woods and the town. The holes and shafts and pitch dark. What it took to build the tunnels and bunkers, what it would take to unbuild them. But there's one part of it I do like: an above-ground, dead-end hollow called Church Cave.

At school they took us to Church Cave on a geography lesson. I remember everything about it, because Miss Bailey was teaching, and she was very encouraging of me and my ideas. She wrote once that I showed a lot of potential. That sort of encouragement's rare. It helps you to learn.

We sat by the entrance to the cave. Miss Bailey was wearing a polka dot dress and a silver butterfly broach. She taught us that the rock quarried in Dark Wood is 169 million years old. It was formed by a shallow sea that evaporated quickly. Miss Bailey taught us about the history of life on planet Earth. She said that if the evolution of life was condensed into a year, and if planet Earth was formed on January 1st, then the first humans existed at four hours to midnight on December 31st, and the first quarrying of these woods occurred at 12 seconds to midnight, which correlates to when the Romans were here. Miss Bailey said, 'Isn't that wonderful? Isn't time a kind of miracle?' But her voice was quiet and frightened.

When you're a child this way of thinking about time helps you to conceptualise history. It helps you see it as big and dark and mostly empty of human influence. But when you get older, I think this kind of conceptualising can be harmful. It convinces you that things slide forward in a chain, one day to the next, one second to the next, and nothing matters but this furious forward movement. Now I see things completely differently. I think of circles overlapping each other, or ripples in a pond, because things repeat. It's a form of arrogance to ignore the repetitions. For instance, bringing the deer to lay to rest in Church Cave, in the woods, where it'll decompose and its nutrients go into the soil and feed the ferns and trees and become bright green cells glowing in the sun. That's a kind of repetition and I'd be arrogant to ignore it.

I approach the cave. A vertical cleft in a small gully, which becomes a corridor with walls of mossy stone. Then it widens into a tall chamber. Above, there's a narrow, deep fissure in the cave roof, cutting all the way out to the ground overhead. Standing there at the right time of day, that fissure lets the light in. It's supposed to be reminiscent of a church, but I used to imagine it was like being inside an enormous egg laid by an ancient creature that a giant had come and cracked open.

I'm tired from carrying the deer. It's fully stiff now and its forelegs drill into my back. I proceed into the cave and breathe the thick, cool air. The temperature contrast from outside is so strong it feels like I've dived into a deep pool. I reach out and touch a wall. Initials are carved into the rock that go back more than two hundred years. I think it's wet, but it isn't, the stone's just very cold.

I must look ugly and strange carrying the deer. Perhaps its stiffness makes it look like a prop, like those tacky Christmas decorations people in town put up on their lawns. I reach the cave chamber, and rest the deer down again, under the tear in the roof. I can't think what else to do with it. I've got nothing to cover it with. I could burn it, and its smoke and ash would plume out the top of Church Cave. But I don't have anything to start a fire.

When Grace's dogs died, she had them cremated and buried the ashes under the beech tree in the back of the garden, specked with dum-dum pellets from where Adam's dad shot at targets with his air rifle. Grace put a nail in the tree and hung up the dogs' old leads. She had some good words of burial. She talked as if she'd lived inside the dogs' heads, as if she'd lived their lives. *You*, she kept saying. *You ran very fast; you chased rabbits in your dreams; you knocked a tooth out trying to attack a moving car*. I think that was the last time I was at Sunrise Cottage.

I look down at the deer's face and I try to visualise its life, from a fawn to this great buck. I imagine it lost its eye in a fight with another buck. I imagine it sleeping under trees in Dark Wood and dreaming about bugs and storms. I try and see the world through its deer-eye, sharp and attentive. I try to imagine the life being sucked out of it, an essence being lifted from it. But I can't.

The cave walls feel tight around me. I can see purple and red flashes in my peripherals and I turn away and clamber out the stone corridor towards the grey door of daylight, pushing my hands against the wet walls for balance and reassurance.

When I get outside, I break into a run up the muddy, root-knotted gully, through the trees and finally onto the main footpath. I step behind the trunk of an oak and pee, and heave, but nothing comes up. I know I need to wash my hands well after touching the deer. I rub them on the tree trunk until they turn red and blood specks start to emerge on my palms like static.

I step back onto the footpath and close my eyes, trying to find the ball of white light glowing behind my sternum. But it's not coming to me, so I start to run again.

The footpath branches off into the cul-de-sac, where Sunrise Cottage is set slightly apart from half a dozen other bungalows. Its long sloped garden runs down to the wood's edge, ending in a part-collapsed plywood fence. The rotary washer's still there in the middle of the lawn, and it's full with white linen.

The gate aches against its hinges as I enter the garden. I stare at the back door and imagine the scene that's about to unfold: my knuckles rapping on its paint-chipped wood, a pillar of lamplight from inside as it cracks open, round red faces plush with private happiness and the promise of new life. I focus very hard on this image.

The back door bursts open. My ears ring. Two screaming children leap out and make me aware of a pulsating white noise, my own thumping blood, by piercing it. The two little boys have mine and Adam's exact likenesses. The little one that looks like me trips and muddies his knees and hands. He gets up, and they both stop dead still and stare gawping at me, stupid as fish.

'Come back inside the house, come here!'

There's a woman standing in Grace's doorway, but it's not Grace.

'Come in now, away!'

She's about my age, a couple of years older. Her black hair's pulled back into a paisley bandanna.

'What do you want?' she says at me, as the little kids move back towards the house. I can see, now, the kids don't look much like me and Adam. For one, Adam's hair was lighter. They both run back inside.

'Is Adam here?' I say.

'Me and my husband live here,' she says.

'This is Grace's house.'

'This is mine and my husband's house.'

I'm beginning to feel angry, because this person's not letting me have much room to explain myself. It's a kind of rudeness I've gotten used to at work. I've learned that many people are predisposed to aggression, and to assume the worst of me. It makes me want to scream, sometimes.

A man appears next to her. He's big and tanned, wearing a grey vest and shorts, in boots that look steel-toed. He has a bushy beard and his mouth is a small oozing red O in the centre.

'Can we help you?' he says. 'You lost your dog or something?'

'No,' I say.

The man approaches me.

'He's looking for some people,' she says, like I'm not even here.

'This is Grace's house,' I say.

'That's the previous owner,' the man says, only a couple of metres from me now, holding up his hands. 'We bought it from her.'

I'm aware my fists are clenched, so much so that the nails are buried into my palms.

'I didn't hear that,' I say.

'That's OK,' he says, 'these things happen. Don't they, darl'?'

The woman walks up to me now, too.

'All the time,' she says.

I look at the exterior of Sunrise Cottage, more closely now. It's precisely how it should be. The moss erupting out of the guttering, ivy eating at the right side of the house. I turn to look at the beech. The dog's leads are even still there. They're so weather-worn they look like part of the tree, green, black and lichen-specked.

'Where'd you come from? You come up the woods?' he says.

'I walked from town,' I say.

'That's long,' she says.

'It's not that long. I took the shortcut.'

'I got to go to town later. I can give you a lift back,' he says. 'You want a drink or something?'

'OK,' I say.

'Sit down if you like,' she nods to three rusted iron-wrought chairs by the side of the house, and steps inside. There's a wooden stool with a fat, full glass ashtray on it. I'm sure it's one of Grace's.

I sit down. At the front of the drive, I can see a white pickup, with a decal that says DREAM ROOFING and a cartoon rainbow stretched between two clouds. The woman reappears and puts a tray down on the bench, with a jug of water and three cups. They sit next to me.

'Sorry about this,' I say.

'Don't worry about it,' he says.

'These things happen,' she says.

He takes out a tin, pops it open, and fills a cigarette paper with dry, gritty crumbs of tobacco. He points the rolled cigarette to me.

'No thanks.'

He shrugs and lights it up. I can smell there's some weed in it.

'I never remember the little details,' she says, 'Like the woman's name. Grace. Otherwise I'd've known right away what you were talking about. You scared me, standing in the garden! All of a sudden I look up, and – you're there!'

'When did they move out?' I ask, casting my eyes down, first to his boots, then to her sandals and toes, which are splattered with white paint.

'Only couple of weeks,' she says.

'House needs a lot of work. Roof repair, floors, kitchen, carpets, electric – '

' – garden,' she interjects.

' – garden, yeah. Painting. All sorts. No offense but the place looked like a museum from 1970 or something.'

Thick smoke cascades from his nostrils. 'You from round here?' he asks.

'Yeah,' I say.

'That's good. We're from round here. My family's been here since back in the 17th century. We got a family tree done and they traced it back.'

'Mine's been here's long as any of us can remember,' she says.

'I never seen you in town,' I say. It comes out coldly but I don't mean it to.

'And I never seen you. So what? Town's getting bigger and bigger. Only notable people there're the characters.'

'The characters,' she repeats, smirking.

I sip from the cup of water.

'Don't mean to be rude but something on you really stinks,' he says.

'It's deer muck,' I say, 'on my trousers.'

'Never heard of no one falling in deer shit,' he says.

'Well, there are deer in these woods,' she says, 'that's true.'

A black cloud covers the sun. The branches of the trees go *rush-rush-rush*.

'I never met her though. The old owner. *Grace*,' she says Grace's name like a foreign word she's unsure how to pronounce.

'No. We come to see the house, two, three times when nobody else is in,' he says.

'Not so strange doing it that way,' she says, 'gives you a chance to think about what you're going to do with it, without feeling's though you're judging the person who's lived there so long.'

'You don't know where they moved to?' I ask.

'No. Why would I?' she says.

Rush-rush-rush.

'Well. You're here now, anyway,' she says.

A dog barks in the woods. He starts to roll another cigarette.

'I remember, actually,' he says, 'I didn't meet the woman. We met her son though. And his missus. The first time we come to view it, they were going out.'

'Adam?' I say.

'If that's his name. Yeah.'

'How was he?' I ask.

'I don't know. How's anyone?'

'It's difficult to say how someone is if you don't know 'em in the first place,' she says.

'Did he seem alright? Did she look healthy, with the baby and everything?'

'I'm sorry mate, I don't know what to say. Like we said we don't know him, or his missus. We must've said about five words to them. How can you judge somebody from that?'

'It's like if I described you,' she said, pointing at me, 'based off this conversation. I couldn't give an accurate description, because I don't know you. It'd just be made-up, by and large. Or if you described us. What could you say? How could you make it accurate? You don't know us!'

We sit there for a while not saying anything. Lethargy comes over me. It's the opposite of the ball of light. It's a bloom, an upside-down mushroom cloud of darkness and heavy mist. It starts in the head and rolls drunkenly down through the body, through the marrow and blood.

'Would you do me a favour?' the man says. 'Would you help me take this in? It looks about to rain.'

He nods at the rotary washer. The sky above is bulbous.

'You can let the kids out, now,' he says to the woman, and she goes in.

The two little boys creep out. One uses my leg to hide behind as though I'm a tree trunk, and shouts, *What's the time Mr Wolf? What's the time?* She follows them out, carrying a plastic washing basket.

I move to the washer and help him unpeg an enormous bedsheet.

'Do it like this,' he says to me, finding two corners on the bedsheet and splaying his arms as far apart as he can.

'It wants to be nice and neat,' she says, watching.

The rain has already started to come down, dotting the cotton with grey blotches. I copy him, and we pull the sheet out so it's huge, tight and flat. We stand there, as if waiting for something to come plummeting from the sky for us to catch.

'Come to me,' he says.

Our hands touch briefly as we match the corners. We step back in unison and touch hands as we match corners again.

'That's it. Do it again,' she says. 'Just like that.'

She grips the basket tightly. Her hands and fingernails are grubby. Like his. Like mine. The clean white sheet with our handprints all over it. Their children in bare feet in the mud in the rain.

'Come to me,' he says. So I come to him.

Kate Crowcroft

—

DOOM

My brother and I used to play Doom. He would give me the code to become invisible. There was a monster in the game we couldn't beat he would follow us through the labyrinth which looked like a corridor. The cheat was Ctrl. Shift. Esc. Pressed at the same time. Pressed down with one hand so the other could be free, so I could move through the floor or the wall he always saved me we only spoke about it once he said: one day I won't be able to save you

(

RE. TRAINING

It was a panopticon I feared, shattering flesh
into bites, bits, to filter stories
with binding pixel spit

    Parcel One
    Classical figure, damaged

I watched the waiters iron & starch their shirts
before their shifts
in the upstairs window of Marion

    Parcel Two
    Female figure, small pieces broken off
    Removed to Box One
    (works very tightly packed)

I ride the train home from the archives,
to the end of the line
& it slips past the final stop into a tunnel

    Parcel Three
    Male figure, protractor set

Last night I dreamt I was saying
good bye, good bye, good bye
to a set of cataract fish eyes

    Parcel Four
    Child's head

I walked the same way I had walked, clutching
my decision to live, and a fire
that caused the sky to thin

Parcel Five
Tools, engraved
Leather pouch, purple lining

Strange alchemy: the smoked sun
took the moon's spectre, became
its inverse twin

Parcel Six
Female figure, and wing

(

YOUR MOTHER'S RIB BREAKS

      like news
      before the world
      weather
            night
            turns
            to night

there is a hurt beauty here that thrives
wild and live
like the skins of things
you never knew
you had inside you
now
    open – *livid* –
spreading blunt, static hue

in desire, I break up, into speech—   )
the colour of flesh contused

      I return the words I hear, as an echo might
      to test, urging – *go* – go on, say more:
      black and blue,
          black
            and blue

Charlie Baylis

—

come as you are

for aaron kent

the opening notes of *come as you are* hover over apricot lakes
precision points shivering on the amp
& your eyes light up
as you are, as you were
in hospital you are dreaming of low clouds
violet dust that gathers around islands
along a line of ribbons
pharaohs study mysterious craters in the desert
what of your own shapes?
are you a damaged tiger?
the wall slides from the phone
by your bedside
(history's great chameleons ruffle your hair
miming
one day you will be ok one day you'll be ok
your brain zipping down clown land
snapping at a million fireflies
like
the study of craters has something to do with shite
& celtic bagels in the mud
sisters of runes who know poetry is a fucking joke
a wild-eyed ponzi scheme   where we lose all
for the price of a shovel
the silhouettes roll slowly down the low land
somewhere you find your anchor
the opening notes of *come as you are* hover over apricot lakes
precision points shivering on the amp
& your eyes light up

inner-peace necklace

in the final days of her life, she wrote to me
about a necklace she had bought for three thousand
dollars at a market stall on the streets of santa clara
in a leafy suburb near the university of santa clara
the necklace had been sold to her as an inner-peace
necklace though it had exhibited no signs of transmitting
therapeutic benefit to anyone in the year
or so she owned the necklace. the situation changed when she died.
she had gifted me the necklace in her will because,
many years ago, i had done her a favour,
a favour she wouldn't want me to tell you about.
so i won't tell you about it. i kept the inner-peace
necklace in a secret place under
my pillow and every morning i would wake up
beside her, beside the dead woman who had given me the necklace,
for a few minutes, then she would vanish.
i can't say much about what happened when we
were together, not being one to kiss and tell, or
not, wholeheartedly, believing in the spirit world, either.   )
what i can say is that as i spent more time with the necklace
i became imbued with a new energy
i found even the smallest speck of dust on the mirror fascinating
the jewels on the necklace were smooth. round and polished
glittering like a chink in a line of cocaine
when i held them in the palm of my hand
the hardships in my life disappeared i saw my fears
were events which had already happened.
nothing to worry about everything would be fine
except the contents of the letter were
quite disturbing. i can't go into detail for
her sake i am protected by her mysterious power
over me i'll try to show you by hints and approximations
the letter really was not quite right, noticeably
not written by someone of sound mind. i
don't know how to tell you perhaps you
have some experience with the mentally ill
the language was not particularly gripping
but there was something haunted in her words
something i couldn't quite place my finger on
the letter was signed willow.

Clare Fisher

—

WTAF

The moon is trending. There is a spider crawling across Sophia's forehead, it is a very small spider; in fact, I'm not sure if it is or isn't a spider, but it is, nevertheless, a creature that she will not want anywhere near her body, she will probably yell at me for not telling her sooner, which I could only do if I were to interrupt her story about her friend's boyfriend and how he sets timers at three-hour intervals throughout the night so that he can 'feed' his avatar in some computer game to which he is unhealthily attached; he hasn't left their flat in months and there is a constant crust at the corners of his eyes, as if he is constantly waking up, Sophie says that her friend says, but if she were to turn off his alarms, he would cry; the friend knows this even though she has never seen him cry, she has never seen any man cry, she is not sure men can cry, which she knows is a cliché, but hey, clichés exist for a reason; and the spider is now on Sophia's cheek and the boyfriend, he has actually stopped going to work, he expects Sophia's friend to pay his rent as well as cook and clean and fetch the gaming paraphernalia he keeps ordering from her – well, it's actually her dad's – Amazon, and every now and then, she thinks: this can't go on, which is exactly what I am thinking re. Sophia's attachment to her friend's boyfriend's attachment to his computer game avatar; she tells me it almost every time we meet, and even when she tells me other things, e.g. the moon is trending, she is telling me it; she is telling me it when she tells me that on the way home from work she saw this massive queue outside this massive warehouse, she thought it was for something really exciting and then she felt annoyed that all the people in the queue knew about it and she didn't, so she joined it, and after what felt like forever but was probably about six minutes, she asked the woman in front what they were all waiting for, and the woman looked at her like she'd said something very rude and she whispered something to the child who Sophia had only just noticed was standing beside her and the child asked what she'd asked and she told them and the child said nothing for what felt like another ever and then they said it's for food and then she said oh and she turned and she moved away from the queue as quickly as she could without running, she didn't want them to think that she hated them, it was more that she hated herself, or something, and the moon is trending, the moon is trending, although how, exactly, can the moon be trending, does it have a Twitter account and who on earth runs it, who on the moon, runs it, more to the – *what*

The actual.

Fuck?

She slaps her cheek. *Was there something on my face?* Her eyebrows crease at an accusatory angle.

No.

I felt something. She slaps it again. *I definitely felt something. But you'd tell me, wouldn't you?*

Of course, I say, and how I feel is like I've snorted a glass of Prosecco, which is how Sophia says her friend says she feels when her boyfriend turns the volume of his console down so low that she hopes, for a second or sometimes two, that it's off.

)

Samra Mayanja

—

SCREAM

Lately I have two voices in my head. The one that I think is my own and the other that is my sister's handwriting.

As I got to the end of the sentence 'If I told you...', I hesitated and dreamt of swimming upwards, up rain droplets, vines, lines, life-lines, charge, frequency, something beginning with lullaby. My sister, whose handwriting I often talk to myself in, had tried to teach me how to swim by teaching me a song. Foolishly I thought it was the song that kept you afloat and almost drowned several times. So much so that she won't talk to me about water.

Now I'm convinced that I could breathe underwater if I tried just one more time.

(Unfortunately, I've learned to be scared of water unless it's vertical streams leading to the clouds, which is the only place I want to be. Specifically this place my sister describes. You take a pin and prick a hole in the cloud when you get there. Then you slip through the hole, where it's apparently silent and the people don't bother you.

When she told me about her hiding place I stopped searching for silence and the thought of it really soothed my mind, soothed me good. What soothes me is the whistling sound as the outside slips through the pin prick and into the cloud. And even if the whistle fills the cloud, I know that we won't drown here.

*

I want to be clear from the start that this story is about juggling a hovering dead body and keeping it afloat with pipes of breath.

So here we go...

I keep hearing that 'breath' is dangerous, the word 'breath' is dangerous. Or is it 'breathe'? Remind me to check that out in the morning. But regardless of the technicalities, it's no harm to a dead man who died of broken lungs, or was it tapping the lungs... or full lungs... or erm his breath hid and then couldn't find its way back out?

It was stuck? Playing hide and seek with his shadow breath. Anyways, he died of something – but the bit that I do remember and the bit that I think about is how his body was floating just above our brows for several days as we argued about where he'd be buried. The whispers in the changing wind is what kept him floating and by whispers I mean tumbling releases of breath. Kept him afloat until there was a grave somewhere for him.

Now the trouble with displaced people is where to bury them; where do you bury those that will meet nobody they know in the soil?

)

Alone.

Perhaps they'll have visitors but only the dead they know can know the dead they know.

So what are we doing? So what do we do then?

People stayed on the phone to tell me they were juggling him, hoping he'd take himself to wherever it was that he wanted to go. Until, well... everything's until.

Until the chiming started and we saw a stranger smoking from the balcony, the light that hit the shadows that hit my cup and when I looked back his eyes were closed but I knew that they were looking into me and I saw everything he knew from beneath the soil.

One lady on the phone asked me once, 'Do you have any ancestors here?' I laughed at that bitch and belted, 'Who doesn't?'

*

Oh, so, they left me running one night, knowing something I didn't and that my breath was short that night. And when I turned away I heard them muttering as though they were close and when I looked once again, they were silent.

I forgot to mention there are no street lights at night, so everyone knows each other by the way they call the other's name. So when I shouted 'family' and they stayed silent I knew that it was because they had decided to flee, but didn't want to take me.

I started digging my own foundations where they'd left me, rather than step back several long strides into an empty house.

Then I felt shuffles, shuffling feet and shuffling hands and shuffling ground beneath me (remember that there are no street lights here and it's still night). As the shuffles grew louder, more pronounced, thorny even, surging out and reaching through my body, I realised that dips of light were dusting the floor. They hadn't left me, the whole world was warming up to dance in our compound. Circles with infinite rings, dancing into and around each other.

With only the soil as our witness whose chest we beat until it was red. We kept dancing.

Dancing for darkness, dancing deep into the soil and dancing so that no one would be alone at the world's end.

Honor Gareth Gavin

—

A Self-Made Man?

Originally written to be read aloud, this piece considers the thickening of my vocal cords on account of HRT testosterone alongside the fluctuating intonations of my dad's radio voice. The URLs included link to recordings of my dad presenting Birmingham radio station BRMB's 'Football Phone-In' in the late '80s/early '90s: found online, uploaded to YouTube by somebody else, these allowed me to use a vocal analyser app to track and visualise the pitch of my dad's retrieved voice at the same time as my present speech. Over the course of the piece, I explore my own disidentifications and gendered aspirations alongside my relationship with my dad's class-based attachment to the narrative of the 'self-made man', a phrase which, in its contemporary adoption by some men of trans history, signals both a knowingness about gender's mutability and, perhaps, a problematic but sustaining fantasy of masculinity as resourcefulness and hard-won success.

—————   )

It's a long time since my dad's heard my voice. For reasons I'll sideline for the time being, we don't often speak, which also means my dad has yet to hear the way in which my voice is beginning to bear an increased resemblance to his. It is and it isn't, that is. As my vocal folds thicken on account of HRT testosterone, absorbed through my skin in the form of a gel with the whiff and consistency of hand sanitiser, my larynx is tilting and my pitch is lowering, but not necessarily steadily and not necessarily consistently. It surges back up, nosedives and cracks. It is this unpredictability, more so than the deepening, that makes my voice feel like a distant memory of my dad's. It is this vocal volatility, brought about by design but not without difficulty, that brings me into awkward intimacy with a voice I have distanced myself from, a voice I haven't heard for a long time – except I have:

G: 'HOLD ON!' George Gavin and Tom Ross – BRMB Football Phone-In, 1987–92: Compilation 3
https://youtu.be/_JHYt3AZ0oc?t=120
[2:00 – 2:07]

That's my dad. By the time that I, a babba assigned female at birth, arrived in his life, my dad was working as a sports DJ for BRMB, Birmingham's local radio station. He grew up on a Kirkby council estate, in Liverpool, an Everton fan. At BRMB he disavowed his Scouse background and loosely identified, though maybe never fully passed, as a Villa man. Somebody at some point has uploaded recordings of him hosting BRMB's Friday night 'Football Phone-In' on YouTube. The tapes date from the late '80s to the early '90s, when my dad was not much older than I am now. It's funny encountering his voice as the object of somebody else's nostalgia, but also gratifying. By registering a stranger's ongoing attachment to him, or at least to the boisterous banter he performed on the show, the recordings relieve me of the burden of interrogating my own ambivalent return to them. I can listen believing it is somebody else whose attention is held by him. I can get back to transitioning, until there it goes again: my voice breaks again, and in the faltering timbre of my own gendered aspirations I cannot help but recognise those of my dad.

(

*

To speak of transition in terms of aspiration is misleading, but also revealing. To do so mispronounces transition's complex modes of self-changing as a trajectory of uplift, a *betterment* that forgets how transness often entails less the ambition of becoming something other than what you are than the desire to leave behind what you never were. But it also gets at the way in which transitioning involves an orientation towards a promise of achievement that might appear as, or even purposely be misrepresented as, a goal. This is a goal, though, that is often only known as such because it has already been felt as an aspect of lived experience, already present in a real and pressing sense. The name for this disjuncture is dysphoria, a source of painfulness that is simultaneously the point at which transness is recruited by the pressures of narrativisation that attend transition into a convoluted yet 'aspirational normalcy' that is also, for some, deeply felt.[1] To get what he wants (hormones, surgery, certificates) from those who hold what he needs (doctors, consultants, therapists, the government), the transmasculine transexual has to convince them that his dream of reinvention is the expression of a life that doesn't require reinventing. Dependency, unbearably feminising anyway, is overwritten by an airtight self-sufficiency, an independence that also conveniently reorientates the promise *inside*, making it his responsibility and his only: *I promise I will become the man I already am*.

I doubt my dad has any idea that many trans men who transition nowadays refer to themselves, in Instagram bios and pin badges and tattoos, as 'Self-Made Men'. I would never – for now; for now, never – call myself a Self-Made Man. I have too many reservations about the way in which the phrase, savvy as it is about gender's social construction, at the same time registers a problematic if sustaining fantasy of masculinity as resourcefulness and hard-won success. But there is, at the same time, a hesitancy in my reservations. Despite them, I am drawn to the phrase and even feel the same awkward intimacy with it that I feel when I listen to the recordings of my dad on BRMB's 'Football Phone-In'. For the self-made man, *making it* means creating a life for yourself on your own terms, against the odds – and if doing so involves, as Lauren Berlant writes, 'the desire to soon experience an imaginary security one knows without having ever had', a desire that might have as its aspired horizon a normativity that for some is already materially assured, discardable instead of prized, then might we not also say, with Berlant, 'fair enough'?[2]

*

I don't know. On the radio, my dad's voice is erratic, excitable, irritable. Sometimes it's low and booming. Other times its fluctuations lace it with a femininity that sits uncomfortably and interestingly with the show's subject-matter and with the bullish irascibility with which my dad addresses those brave enough to follow the suggestion of the show's name and *phone in*. Here he is having a go at Bernard from Liverpool, my dad's disavowed hometown that nonetheless sometimes, if you listen close enough, lets itself be known in his phonemes and vowels:

G: George Gavin and Tom Ross – BRMB Football Phone-In,
1987–92: Compilation 3
https://youtu.be/_JHYt3AZ0oc?t=130
[2:10 – 4:51]

Already by this point in his career he has washed and softened his Scouse accent to the extent that it bears hardly any resemblance to the way my Nana and aunties all spoke, but it surfaces in certain words still, and his swaggering dismissal of Merseyside is likewise touched by a knowingness that he might be in the process of giving himself away, or up. I can tell he is enjoying the joke. He introduces callers, interrupts, cuts them off:

G: George Gavin and Tom Ross – BRMB Football Phone-In,
1987–92: Compilation 3
https://youtu.be/_JHYt3AZ0oc?t=651
[10:51 – 11:17]

(

The energy of the show is do or die. Grab your opportunity by the bollocks or get lost. There's a cruelty to it that is also exhilarating, an agitation and impatience that maybe has a way of referencing, in tempo and tone, the 'improvisatory opportunism' and surrealism of persistence that marks social mobility when the path up and out is not obviously mapped.[3] For the self-made man, though, *making it* is a genre whose precarious and undependable conventions of fulfilment often paradoxically culminate in an insulated individualism, one that retroactively elides material conditions of opportunity and instead emphasises the sheer force of self-determination: *I always was the man I have become*. But then, who would or could blame him? Why do you want to be around these people? I once asked my dad, at a party with canapés in the countryside a million miles away from either Erdington, Birmingham, or Kirkby, Liverpool. Because I'm as good as they are, he answered. Fair enough.

It's a funny thing, turning my own academic practices of close reading back on passages of my dad's local radio show, the sonic environment of my youth. I speak a different language now. Grammar school and a career in higher education have almost completely emptied my own voice of its Brumminess, though my gone accent still contours the rhythms of my prose. I have to work hard not to write sentences that sound singsongy. I like writing sentences that sound singsongy. Sometimes I wonder if the singsongyness is still there in my spoken voice, an undertow that feminises it even as it drops. As a kid, I famously did a number on BRMB singing Twinkle Twinkle Little Star in a high-pitched Brummie voice. The recording of *that*, thank god, is lost.

*

For some self-made men, the fact that their gender has had to be worked for and fought for ultimately secures for them a masculinity that is more masculine than masculinity itself. And yet the logic underscoring this is eloquently confessional of masculinity's tenuousness, the fact that it can be taken on and stripped off. HRT makes you understand that gender is as much about *maintenance* as it is about being, or becoming, or performing, or anything else. Maybe this is something femininity already knows all too well, but there is also a sense in which transitioning brings you into close and sometimes discomforting proximity with gender's means of subsistence, with what it takes to wake up in the morning with a sexed body at all. One definition of privilege is the possibility of keeping a bit of distance from the more wearing, less visible activities of social reproduction. In this sense, non-exogenous (or 'naturally' produced) testosterone is for cismen what domestic labourers are for the middle classes. Or perhaps that's a facile comparison. After all, once it is circulating in your bloodstream, it doesn't matter where the testosterone has come from, whether it originated in your balls or in a bottle of Testogel 1.62%. Testogel as a product, a commodity and object of exchange, is made and marketed for cismen anyway too. In *this* sense, the difference between cismasculinity and its trans counterpart recedes, revealing a shared dependency on a resource-cum-commodity whose extraction and abstraction is itself the legacy of a long history of the body's compartmentalisation, the production of the 'body-in-parts'. This is a history that, as Jordy Rosenberg has shown, includes the fates of the vagrant and incarcerated and criminalised, early modernity's outliers of capitalism whose hung and drawn corpses were appropriated by the burgeoning medical profession and dissected as territories of experimentation, if they weren't packed off to the colonies to do the dirty 'work of dispossess[ion]' there first.[4] In other words, class and transsexualism are longstanding bedfellows, but in complex and sometimes unexpected ways.

In the language of transness, to *go stealth* is to go undeclared in the world. It is to not name yourself openly, or not everywhere, as trans. *Stealth* for some is the dream, the point at which the work and the waiting and the painfulness will all have been worth it. But simultaneously, stealthiness subtracts the belaboured backstory that partly produces its value: like the polished commodity-form forgets the labour that it has taken to make it, to *go stealth* is to render the process of getting there no longer present, no longer perceptible, scurried away. For some, for sure, it is a mode of survival, a relief from the endlessly interrogated burden (in some places and some contexts) of being visibly trans. But it is also a dream of achievement that is often minimally available to those who don't already have the social and economic stability to ease its coming-into-being.

G: DON'T YOU EVER!
https://youtu.be/O1FYS_Z5bQk
[0.00 – 0.55]

Over the course of writing this I've drifted significantly from my dad's disembodied voice, or maybe I was never wherever it is. Every communication, whether written or spoken or both as with this one, has a way of keeping something to itself. Every communication keeps a secret whilst also being the only way that the secret is felt. This (for me anyway) is both the pleasure and difficulty of communicating at all; more often than not, you come up against something you didn't set out to say. Though I'm drawn to the recordings of my dad's voice uploaded to YouTube, as it is, I can't listen for long. The reasons for this are both near and far to me, so I'll keep them sidelined for now. But what I can say, having written this, is that my aversion to listening is also the broken home of my reluctant yet resolute affinities: it's my feeling of needing to get away from the volatilities of his voice that helps me understand the persistence of my attachment to them, and maybe to understand something about him too. Or at least, to imagine that I do.

—

[1] Lauren Berlant, *Cruel Optimism* (Durham, NC and London, Duke University Press, 2011), p. 170.
[2] Ibid., p. 180.
[3] Ibid., p. 41.
[4] Jordy Rosenberg, 'Trans/War/Boy/Gender: The Primitive Accumulation of T', *Salvage* (21 December 2015), available at https://salvage.zone/in-print/trans-war-boy-gender.

)

Joe Carrick-Varty

—

from *sky doc*

Once upon a time when suicide was scaffolding for the sky

        all the silence the countless times my dad

        slammed the door forever after a row

        with my mum have you ever heard a house

        exhale for the duration of a weekend

        just the cats padding the landing

        my mum smoking cross legged on the lawn

(when she stood again how tall she looked

Once upon a time when suicide was the answer to the question

        when a tree falls in my forest of memories

        and no one else hears it has it happened

        suicide purring wants to know the answer

        to a different question tell me

        if a room of dead dads and a room

        of dead rappers fell from the same height

        which room would reach the ground first   )

Once upon a time when suicide was choosing the wrong friend

    to be honest with at a house party

    in year 11 and how that friend

    not my best but certainly not my worst

    never quite looked me in the eye again

    on the topic of always saying too much

    suicide pulls up a plastic patio chair

    envelopes me in the booziest hug

(

Once upon a time when suicide was rain that gathers

    and protects its own darkness

    I once told my mum I believed

    I was a murderer she was

    coming out of the toilet

    of course believing and being

    are two different things suicide

    pockets a star promises me unlimited wishes

)

                                                                                                                     .

Joe Carrick-Varty

Once upon a time when suicide was two schools of thought

    the borderline heroic tried very hard

    just couldn't take it anymore

    or the selfish but how could you

    someone would have to find you

    the best way of explaining suicide to anyone

    was a drawer I opened one morning

    full of my dad's old elastic bands

(

Once upon a time when suicide was an hourglass

        tipped on its side that old cliché

        about love and knowing where to look

        what if I told you my dad still

        crosses the street some Sundays

        wearing the same Helly Hansen

        his body stopped breathing inside of

        and always it's me he doesn't recognise

)

Emily Hasler

—

Course

This morning the still river served up
a surplus of shelduck, so many my mind
ran fowl—chewing over their muddled taste.
The gullet has a canniness beyond the brain's.
I was caught with feathers round my gills,
gristle in my evolvéd teeth. For starters,
I forced down that guilty mouthful: gritgrit.
I want to eat what the river gives me. It gives me
assiette of dirts (locally sourced when available).

(

A Mud

is a singular creature
of variable size
with a great many mouths.

It can smack and suck its lips
but mostly stays schtum,
sticks around quietly.

It adores a Water,
and they mingle parts
twice daily,

then roll away and lie
prone and touching,
the scent of each rising

into an Air (a whole other story).   )

Edward Doegar

—

from *I never thought it would come to this*

vi.

The trick of perspective
Seems such
An innocuous reason
For revolution

How like a god
To think of that then
Hardly exactly true
And yet

(

Something remains
Of the first time
We met unexpectedly
Awkward

Sharing perhaps
As if it were a substantial
Meal
Giddy with discovering

But also
Obvious as cardamom
And rose
Lemon and parsley

vii.

Belief is organised
By what we see
Through
These carceral lines
Our mind

Mistakes
Aggregation and agreement
The plural world
Made comprehensible
By cause

Because
Organised in belief   )
We see by whom
We are seen
To acknowledge

Labour
As means of faith
In change
Multiplying affect
Into effect

What I'm getting at
Escapes me
Is of no consequence
And cannot matter
But vote

viii.

Me telling you
The only thing that truly matters is

This understandable expectation
That pervades the ethic of

The child within
Meaning one thing removed from

Another violent disbelief
The process of releasing oneself from

(

The settled argument
Present in the sense that disappoints

ix.

Who knows what possibility
Possesses a fact
Jealous of the future

Of stage thunder
The cannon ball bowled across the heavens
Importing

Without second thoughts
With what threatens to be a premonition
I think

Doom is on its way)
The coming scene where you are already
Altered into that you

That is lost
In understanding
Knowing I can't speak to you anymore

Edward Doegar

x.

Violating dust

Not subject and yet

Subjected to

Laws that rust

The will of the people

(

The poems from this sequence were written so that the stanzas could be arranged in any order. The arrangement presented here was chosen by the editor. The twenty-poem sequence responds to a print series of the same name by the artist Jamie George. Other poems from this sequence can be found in recent issues of *The Poetry Review*, *Perverse* and *Tentacular*.

Victoria Manifold

—

Daytrippers

We waited for the bus for almost a full hour and I was soaked wet right through to me knickers. Mammy and nan were wetter, somehow, and Terese and Siobhan were about the same wet as me. Da wasn't even there so was dry somewhere I would've thought.

Hot too probably, fire turned up to four bars, having one of those miniature cigars with the smell, smiling because we were all gone out on this day trip without him and he could watch the football or whatever it was that he liked, something with sports or a police detective or with the young women in the tight dresses all breathless like and waiting.

But now the bus was stuck somewhere between Grunne and Gordt and there was no shelter for us as we waited, and the rain wouldn't stop. Nan's fags were going out as soon as she lit them, the paper on them falling apart, just dissolving like that and the baccy crumbling wet to the pavement in awful clumps, useless, and still the bus not coming.

The other people waiting with us were getting wet too, were starting to grumble and moan, starting to look at us as if it was our fault. Mammy saying to me 'get under me coat' but under the coat it was also wet. Nan saying to Siobhan 'you get under here too' and opening her coat up. Terese having to take it all without another person's coat to get under because she was older and must be a big brave girl.

And she is a big brave girl, standing in the rain, as she sees, after all this time, the bus coming up over the hill and her face is beaming in a smile and she says 'the bus, the bus is here' as if she had made it happen with her powers, as if she is someone else after all.

The bus sprays us with a wave of gutter water as it pulls up, sprays it right into our little faces and it tastes like dirt but we lick our lips, happy because we are going out on this day trip. We are leaving behind Gordt for the day, leaving behind the smell from the chicken processing factory, leaving behind the sharp angled boys who travel over from Grunne to tease us in their blazers and shoes.

The driver presses a button to open the door with a sound like breathing out. He sits up high in his low visored cap, the blue reflecting on to his rough face so that we cannot see his eyes, only a navy shadow that covers half his face and his red hands are gripping the giant steering wheel.

He tells us all to hurry up and get on, get on the bus now now now, no time to waste, but people are pushing us out of the way to get there before us, they're all trying to be first, trying to get the best seats and they're leaving me and Siobhan and Terese to squeeze into one seat together, which is not fair, which is not how I wanted it to be when mammy said we were going on this day trip.

Mammy is saying 'no whinging Alanna, you can sit on Terese's knee.' But I am not a baby to be put on Terese's knee and the tears prick at the backs of my eyes, the choke comes in the throat.

'We're having a nice trip out, so no crying, no showing me up, no making a show of yourself in front of all these people.'

But I cannot help it, the tears are on my face now, are dripping from my chin now, and people are looking at mammy and shaking their heads. So of course Siobhan – who is not like me, who is a good girl all the time – goes on Terese's knee and I get to sit on the seat, right near the window, with mammy and nan in front of us in their own seats.

My wet legs are rubbing against the rough carpet of the bus upholstery, an itch comes that is unbearable, that is a spiked worm burrowing in all over my thighs, that is surprising in how it strikes so sudden, so that all I can do is jump up from the seat, all I can do is squirm and prance about. And then mammy is starting in on me again, all hushed and angry saying 'Alanna, Alanna sit down, Alanna I'm ashamed of you.'

It is always me that these things happen to, only yesterday mammy had said we might not even go on the day trip, that I might have ruined it all for everyone because there was a dead dog in the fields out the back of our house and I said we should go and see it. It was lying there with its eye kicked out and all this terrible jelly on it and when I poked it with a stick something wet oozed out onto my shoes, the little white plimsolls I love so much. The wet was dark and thick.

Mammy had seen the shoes when we got in and we had to tell her all about the dead dog. She shouted at da 'Craig, phone the fucking Council, the bairns have touched a dead dog.' Da just looked at her and said 'What are the Council going to do Shannon? They've already touched it now. Will the Council turn back time, Shannon?'

But mammy dialled the number anyway and listened to the recorded message they played, a lady's voice saying 'Due to the ongoing amalgamation process your call cannot be answered at this time, please hang up and try again later… Due to the ongoing amalgamation process your call cannot be answered at this time, please hang up and try again later…' over and over.

'I suppose you'll ring Scott now,' da said and mammy stared at him with her lip moving all trembly like. We were not supposed to say the name Scott in our house but when, sometimes, it slipped out of mammy's mouth da would not be happy for a while. I had not heard da say it before and now when he did mammy moved in a way that made me think of a little bird.

And then mammy and da sat quiet for a long time, mammy with tears on her cheeks. A big wet-faced grimace which made me think we're probably going to die, we touched the dog and now we'll die and mammy is crying because she's thinking about our little coffins.

But mammy dried her face and said 'if you do anything else then we're not going on this day trip anymore. Now get up in the bath and be good.' So, we washed ourselves clean of the dog and anything else, all in the bath together, me and Siobhan and Terese. Then we sat still and quiet under the big clock with the spikes like sun rays coming out of it. The clock ticked and ticked, the clock counted down the seconds until we could wait for the bus, until we could all stand together in the rain.

Now I am looking out of the window and the bus is full of fumes, all sick-making, all light-headed now, but I can't complain because mammy might cry again and nan might smack my legs. I have to be good now like Terese or Siobhan, like all the other kids when they come to school with pencil cases and lunchboxes, hair tied in ribbons and all that.

At the zebra crossing there is a tiny woman eating, with her hands, a massive steak – blood dripping down onto her top which is very light, almost white. She is so little and the steak so big that she needs both her hands to hold it and between bites she is licking her lips. And the steak is getting wet with the rain and her hair is getting wet too but she doesn't seem to mind, just carries on tearing at the meat with her teeth. She crosses over and the bus drives on but when I crane my neck back to look at her, I can see her light top is full soaked in the blood of the steak and the wet of the rain.

Terese and Siobhan didn't see her because they have their heads together and are talking in quiet voices to each other. They will not include me, they didn't want to go and see the dog yesterday, they didn't want to poke at it and touch it and see the dark wet of it. Now they don't want to look out of the window with me, don't want to see the same things I am seeing, do not want my badness to rub off on them.

We pass the field where there are still one or two cows left and the big house mammy sometimes cleans at. The man and woman there are called Daphne and Michael but they make mammy call them Mr. and Ms. Eastman, 'yes Mr. Eastman, yes Ms. Eastman', she is always saying to them. They always call her Shannon or, sometimes, Sharon. I heard them saying this to her, calling her the wrong name, because she was allowed to take me with her as long as I was quiet and stayed outside. But then the thing started happening with the cows and I wasn't allowed to go anymore. Mammy said 'no you can't go, look at what has happened to the cows up there.' Daphne and Michael had come from a big city somewhere else, but they never go back there now. They only stay in their house in Grunne, watching through their big windows what is happening to the cows in their field. And sometimes, instead of watching the cows, Daphne might cry and shake a little bit but Michael never does.

As we drive down the high street, people come out of shops to wave at us. They've strung bunting across their awnings and inflated some angular balloons. All the people of Grunne seem to have come out to watch the bus, like they have never seen one before, although they run every day to Gordt and back. This is not quite like the other buses though. This is a special bus, only for day trips.

On this bus there is a little toilet like a cupboard and I must go, even though I am scared, even though it's down some steps and you must be so low, so close to the road moving so fast. But mammy comes with me and holds me in place, afterwards saying 'don't wipe that way you'll get shite in your fairy and it'll go bad' and I know she isn't angry at me for crying anymore.

Now we are happy again, thinking of the day trip, thinking of how we will be somewhere else for a little while. When we get there, there will be bright pink sticks of peppermint rock, there will be grey sand sticking in clumps to our ankles and calves, there will be battered cod and hot chips turning the paper they're wrapped in see-through with grease. Terese will wear a new bikini and Siobhan will wear the one Terese wore last year and I will wear the one Siobhan wore last year and Terese wore the year before and the pink rock will turn gummy in our wet mouths, filling in the spaces between our teeth.

The sea will be dark, vast. And the sky dark also. Nan will sit in her striped deckchair and smoke one fag after another, putting them out on our sandcastles, calling them flags, calling it pageantry, calling us babies for crying about it. And mammy will still be worried but less worried than at home. She will eat an ice cream and smile once or twice.

And might da even miss us when we are there? Might he be crying into the little lotions and potions on mammy's dressing table later? Might he hold a soft worn teddy bear to his face and repeat our names?

But we are still miles from the sea, still on the bus and the rain is closing in on us in grey coloured walls. I think maybe we are further away than when we started. The wipers don't work like they should, there is no fresh air now, only our breath steaming up the windows and the smell from the little toilet. I cannot see outside anymore, cannot see Grunne or Gordt or anywhere else. I am still wet right through to me knickers and there's no hope of me ever getting dry again.

(

Robert Casselton Clark

from *Scripts*

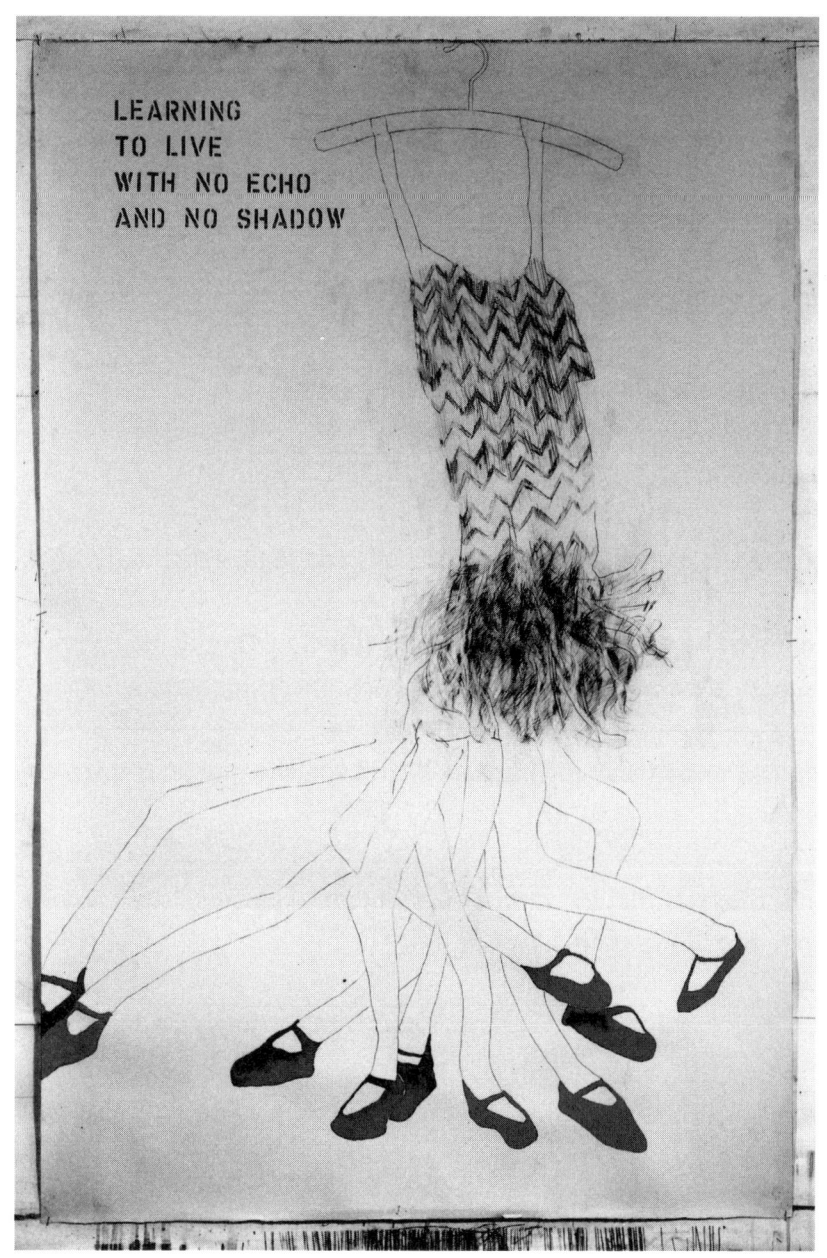

DRAWING

An itch of it vibrates about a bit, in the raw, on the white-out sheet.

Look:

Crossings-over and crossings-out.

A convolvulus traction.

Fowled tremulousness.

All jet and slicked back. Remember?

Fingerprints pushing a quiver across organ keys.

It's touched.

(It breathes, it comes alive with loads of little legs, wrigglingly.

A signing in the sand, all along the high-tide line. One ripple so precisely delineated, then another, and another, on unfurling scrolls.

Lifting way away from any line, so. With luck, the line goes untraceable places.

To glide the next instant through a moment's passing, when no one's looking, into alone time.

THE GALLERY

A superb opportunity has arisen. All mod cons. Open plan. An internal viewing is essential.

There is life here, but not as we know it.

Could loneliness be a friendship with the dead?
A spinebone cleavage of 'me' and 'we'.

Look at that one, look at that one, look at that one. PUT A POND IN IT, see what happens, turn into a loon, then leave.

Mutations take place.

The afterimages echo and echo, in secrets.

Secreted.

)

'You're not going to become melancholy again, are you?'

My lighthouse, having blown its stained-glass, levitates rainbows.

FILM (MATINÉE)

It's a thing with its shadow all awander.

One so-and-so meets up with another so-and-so in a mood for suddenly disappearing.

The air is activated with hushed expectancy and heavenly intervenings.

Eyes rolled, eyes raised, blinkered in flickers, blushing dark good looks.

Keyholes.

Crystal chandeliers.

A car revving in reverse.

An alarm clock ticking.

A bracelet.

A suitcase, uncollected, revolving.

That trembling in the floor.

That aghast, and the ghost of it.

Kneeling in the rain, 'Words have eaten me,' she says.

Jessa Mockridge

—

SWIM

Ok. Eyes! Eyes! Eyes! I want to go quickly now. There's a dark tunnel ahead. Wide. Wide enough for a car. It's hard to see how deep. Knees. Knees. Thigh. Crotch. Ankle. Knees. Knees. Knees. I – against the rush of water. The motorway bridge – the tunnel – at Lewisham. It's deep. Around the sides, I think. It's dark. The phone! I've got this crap phone at least. Dim though. It's dim. Water, rushing. Water rushing, fast. Traffic rushing. Dark. Knees. Ok. In the water – there are – sticks. On the sticks. On the – ghwoop! Gaaargh brr shit. Alright. Alright. Stones. Yes, stones. They hold, rushing. Up to the waist. No signal on the thing now. Fish jumping. Limbs jumping. Hammering. It's fine. It's fine. You're good. You're good where you are. There it is! There's the end. Right there. Not too dark. Deep though. Waist deep. Stinks. Stinks like rot. A fish! A big fish! Here, follow it. Follow it with the torch. The edge is good. Over the mulch. Just the feet. The tunnel coils round. Follow. Rushing. Birds. Concrete. That buzzing, drilling. And voices. Loud. Swampy. Rotting. Disgusting rotten dead things. Dead things in here. Wide though. Very wide. There's air. There's air.

The tide is rising. It's one year. Now the huge gates of Limehouse lock finally open to meet the wide River Thames. Immediate wind rushes metre-high waves downstream. Salt spray whips my face. Shining water extends oceanically as far as I can see in both directions. I feel my body itself open and extend. I. Am. Immense. My being in water is planetary: the waves, this river, the wind, the restless sea, the positions of the sun and moon and Earth, connecting canals, the weather, the rain, blood through the body, the atmosphere, aquatic algae and slime moulds, gravity, tears, ancient glaciers, fizzy drinks, treated water through pipes and pumping stations, piss, snowmelt, sick in a clogged-and-slow-draining public sink, vast pink salt lakes. A whole year! I can't feel where my numb limbs end and the cold water begins.

Blood beats through the body, amplified underwater. When I come up for air the surface is carpeted in thick green duckweed. I wipe the scum off with both hands and feel weak sun on my face. Hello? Hi, is that you? Slow eyes follow the swift voice. There's my manager standing in a stiff fitted dress and blazer in front of the sewage ventilation tower at Mile End Park. A low railing cordons off the tow path from a field of new grass and little white-faced daisies. Looks very refreshing! Light bounces off weeds like velour. Listen, the library has been really busy with the start of term and I appreciate your work so far. But if you could please keep logging into Libchat daily.

Arms. Legs. Arms. Legs. Breath. Saturated clothing swells and twists in heavy canal water. With unfeeling fingers I peel off wide jeans and shapeless black hoodie. Windows and windows like walls of security monitors on a punishing dimming day. The work phone, in a ziplock bag, rings out urgent notifications when a student requires attention. It's three months. I pass Salmon Lane Lock with its ugly futuristic footbridge. Past the tall tower block the canal widens, pond-like. Geese and green-headed ducks are pink this electric evening, washing and fishing for bits to eat.

(

A flat pink silicone star cleaves to the plughole with suckers on the underside of each point. Holes on its surface still drain thick water from a just-had shower. The star-shaped plate offers a collection of trapped twisting body hairs held flat beneath a heavy scented froth. I pluck and plug and let the hot tap run as hot as it goes. I want to say something about the water purification process. How most drinking water in London comes from upstream the Thames. Rainwater sloshes into rivers and streams and swells groundwater. It's pumped. It's stored. It's settled. It's screened. It's filtered through sand. It's chlorinated. And here it comes! Hot! In the street, notice the small square drain covers that say 'water' or 'Thames Water' outside each house. This is where treated water flows in and splits to reach toilet, shower, bath, boiler and sink.

The full height of the tide is marked by a film of sea algae up the brick embankment, the scum ring of the falling river. I cling onto a thick wooden beam that lines the artificial bank. The tributary is wide and strong and rushing out to sea. Muddy banks rise up and fold like gums.

I claw my way up the creek – the press of my palms, knees, shins and backs of my feet on mud – just far enough to feel the heft of my grounded body more than the forever suck of the river. I drop half out, half in, fully exhausted. Clusters of people behind black safety railings eat sandwiches, rest against bikes, look to the sunset. They amble along the waterfront and over the footbridge across. A managed row of trees begins to shed brown leaves.

The pipe spits me out in a narrow ditch between two wooden fences. It's all sharp edges! Dry sharp sticks. Scraping. Dusty wire mesh, coiled, springy. Piercing. Slabs of stony concrete, broken rubble. Grazing. Frayed burned rubber. Burning. Blue scrunched tarpaulin. Stinging. Backs and legs of disused institutional furniture; chairs, mostly. Bruising. Hard wood soft with water rot. Rubbing. Dirty foil and tin plates crumpled, balled. Squashing. Sheets of milky crisp plastic. Blistering. Red corroding dismantled scaffolding. Prickling. Throbbing. Men dig this narrow ground channel afraid of water. They install a trash screen here. Still water is known to spill. To cover landscaped gardens. To seep beneath doors of houses. Saturate carpets and flood gleaming floorboards. How to recover after a flood? Contact your insurance company. Wooden fence slats are poster-paint green with moss and fat muscley trees thrust into a very blue sky.

Night buses disturb dark, biting swill at my knees, below the shrill motorway at Deptford Bridge. My thighs stick and chafe. It's weird. Having a body after swimming for so long. I'm not walking again, no. It's not like it was. I've never even been here and I can't feel the feet at all! Snow specks fall like dandruff on white polyester into the river. Cold cement walls of the culvert are taller than me, with iron safety-railings on top. They match the grey underbelly of the raised DLR tracks, with a lacquer of slime and graffiti. It's quite nice, this. Not having to decide to stay in the water, again, today. I wouldn't be able to. I don't think – I'd be able to climb out of here if I wanted to. The river, the creek, the Thames, the canals, keep going day night day night day. It's simple. Waterways have junctions and tunnels; curve and skirt through cities and towns with sharp bends and locks; open onto basins; meet large rivers; flow out to sea; fork into creeks; split into tributaries; are lost to modern waste water systems. It's not easy but at least I actually know which way to go!

Waves withdraw to unmoving puddles and I begin to crawl up the shallow creek. Fingers web with used wet wipes. I don't get a drink I don't get bed I don't get a hot bath I don't get a hot meal I don't get to sleep and sleep and sleep. *I'm tired*, I whine at stupid muck. The muck says nothing. The muck is pocked with sharp bottle caps, plastic bottles, wrappers, Styrofoam cups, rude takeaway boxes, bloated lifeless fish and small scuttling crabs. They crunch beneath tender knees and hands. The clear sky makes it very cold and the moon is a waxing gibbous, whatever that means. I crawl past a shopping centre, under a motorway, by rusted boats precarious and permanent sitting on mud, past premium private housing, in between industrial estates, motor repairs and Greenwich Pumping Station. Deep, deep underground this is where the hidden tributaries of three sewage flows intercept. Shit and cooking fats slowly slide through downward sloping pipes: from Herne Hill through Peckham and New Cross; from Balham, through Clapham, Stockwell, Brixton and Camberwell; and from Putney through Battersea to Vauxhall and Bermondsey. They are pumped back up to the surface, combined and moved on to be treated. Bacteria in oxygen-free containers digest plant and animal and human waste emitting methane – or wait – let's call it biogas! Apple trees and low-growing food crops bloom from dried-sludge composting soil. Piss powered battery recharging for phones and cars is already a thing! Before wastewater was literal energy it was wastewater. The ground vibrates. My body vibrates. Metres below surface, below clay, a huge industrial drill named Annie (after the suffragette) breaks through the shelly layer that before now had been undisturbed for millions of years. Thames Water, a large private company, is building London's New Super Sewer. Waste water, water treatment, water supply, waste water, water supply and demand: Thames Water. Sites were shut for just three weeks despite the deadly virus. Of course the priest blessed the Tunnel Boring Machine. There's the plastic relic of Saint Barbara to protect miners from sudden and violent death at work.

The doctor gives me the number for my local treatment service. It keeps ringing and ringing. Tory cuts mean more people hospitalised.

More people killed. Thick clear plastic tube down the throat. Sharp all the way to the stomach. Gagging. Further. Coughing. Now flooded. Cold. Vomiting. Vomiting. Never vomited cold before. Into a bucket, yes. Retching. Now nothing. Now charcoal. Literal charcoal. Pumped full of the horrible black stuff. Soak up toxins. Heaving. Now the tube comes out. I've never had a voter come up to me and say we should spend more money on alcohol treatment services, the council's deputy leader says.

Sunlight bounces off the crystal stream, bright green and brown. The green is the bright green of algae. Tall trees and a stone wall surround the river. I feel my feet! Banks slope steeply to water, covered in thorny brambles, strewn with stained toilet paper, ivy, cartons, delicate butter flowers and an abandoned baby car-seat. A church and footpath on the left. Fields of water-thick lawn on the right. It's sunny! It's warm. A small stream feeds into the fast-moving river. I follow it and the silly daffodils under a footbridge. Daffodils! Like joke drawings of flowers that inexplicably swelled and became flowers! They might squirt you with their frilly trumpets! I'm blinking in birdsong and child song and song song of this actual sun. My pinking body is porous and panting as a tongue. Young families are out walking today. Don't be fooled though! This green space is not recreational. Open earth soaks rain. Stops groundwater from filling sewers. Stops sewers spilling, raw and untreated, into rivers and oceans. I leave a wake of grease and gunk in clear water past the tennis courts, playground and the twirly bridge over the railway tracks.

The gate, two colossal steel crescents against the powerful tidal water, is shut. I haven't booked twenty-four hours in advance. Have to wait for opening times to call Aquavista when a team of volunteers is on site. My throat and mouth are dry. What I need is a nice cold drink. I could climb out right now. It's low tide. I tread water. It's high tide. Sun rises. I tread water. Just a few stragglers left kicking discarded tins, hoping to find something unopened. Salt water pulls on tired panties and t-shirt. My mottled flesh is exposed and cyan when the sun pokes out between morning clouds. It's opening hours but tidal locks depend on the tide. It's just before low tide. Limehouse Lock doesn't open two hours either side of low tide. I tread water. It's low tide. A student is trying to get hold of an article the library doesn't have access to. I'm a library worker so I can't recommend illegal sites like https://sci-hub.yncjkj.com. Make sure to use a VPN or ask me how! I tread water.

Water safety: don't! God's sake – it's summer. Don't risk it? Depth perception. Canals are often shallow which you can't always tell from the surface. Friends will think that's boring. If I jump in or try to swim I might hurt myself on the rough canal floor. Christmas is coming and not all canals are shallow, they can also get really deep. If I can't put my feet on the ground it'll be difficult to get out. Then it's New Year's, obviously, there'll be hidden dangers: reeds and other plant life could tangle around my limbs and trap me. Rubbish lurks below the water. I could cut myself on broken glass or get snagged by a rusty bike or trolley just in time for my birthday. Disease: my sores and scratches would open me to waterborne diseases. Imagine the holidays: cold shock. Waterways can be colder than they feel. I wouldn't be able to write. Cold would rush blood away from muscles to protect the organs and the muscles would cramp. I could drown. If I'm unemployed, a migrant, under-age or under the influence, police will refuse to enter the water. Don't stay in the water.

A morning canopy of little red berries falls over rushing water. I like that 'rapid' is how the water's moving, quick! But it's also the thing itself: a rapid. The loud gush gives this body energy. The water is clean! I can see Citibank's hot salmon data centre now. It's crashing, falling. There are plants growing inside the culvert. Sediment blooms with each dragging step. Water holds sand and silt, suspended, before it's rushed downstream. Here on the North Sea bed sediment settles, becomes cemented, becomes rock. Moving from one place to another: erosion. I'm thinking about trespassing. The enclosing walls of the chute don't feel trespass-y. This feels public. I keep left. Still with the sensation, from years of vibrating conditioning moving through this city, that someone might pass me briskly. There's graffiti on the concrete walls: EXMA, PARA, KUSH, CKONE. I like thinking of whoever drew these lines being here in the water too. Here. Here's someone's place. A tent up. Under the bridge.

On the riverside opposite, uniform white-bottomed newbuild apartments are tiny between choppy water and demanding sky. It feels good and frightening for my depleted body to be moved into this large expanse of wild water. I kick hard and push the arms through the resistant and quick river. The powerful rising water of the North Sea has me. Rain begins pelting down in sheets. There's not enough green space in concrete London to slow the stormwater so even light rain like this fills sewers right up. Thirty-two million tonnes of raw shit gushes directly into the Thames from fifty-seven combined sewer overflow outlets. Rapid waves dunk me under the oil and sewage-full tidal river. Arms and legs useless against the current – I let go. Of direction. Of home. Of bearings. The head above water is everything. Water, wind, rain, countless bodies lost before, carry me, untethered, far, far up the toxic river.

Crisp sparkling cider. Fizzing gin and bitter tonic. Lime apple white wine. Smooth vanilla hops. Shock of salt tequila. Sugar smack of anise and elderberry. Dark thick milk ale. Deep warming pepper red. Hot lemon honey rum... It's twelve days, I can't get enough bottles to keep going during lockdown. It's four months, my residence is denied by a racist office clerk. It's four weeks now and my mother can't recognise me anymore. Belly pain constipation bloating cramps gas; my first year without drink is the first year with my gut. This week I have a gas leak in my house – the thought of anything happening to the boys! It's two months, I don't answer the door or leave the house except for these meetings. A friend drives me to treatment and my husband takes our kid to school, the first month. I stay with my auntie while I get electroshock therapy. I ask for tea at The Bird's Nest. Right, I actually drink *for* my mental health, the man says looking cross. My skin is furrowed and slick with thick oil and silt, a welcome layer against stone air. I stuff Twiglets into my dry mouth with a tepid sluk of weak tea. Thick water is rising again: covers my soft calves, warmer than night. Find anything good down there? He presses his face to the bars straining to see the dark wet passage. I dig into mud with my toes; clasp it, claw-like, dangle it and fling it to settle and slowly sink back into gloop. Urgh gross! Wet wipes. The creek bed is basically made of wet wipes.

Jessa Mockridge

On YouTube you can listen to eight hours of TOILET FLUSH SOUND EFFECT, TOILET SOUND, eight hours of Toilet ASMR, Toilet Flushing Noise, Water Flush. In the bathroom cupboard there are body condiments in squirt and twist top bottles. I take a sploosh of each: Herbal Essences argan oil repair shampoo, fruity pineapple and papaya shower gel by Superdrug, fruity strawberry and raspberry shower gel by Superdrug, fruity watermelon and pomegranate shower gel, fruity blueberry and acai shower gel, fruity orange and satsuma shower gel, a massage soap that smells like cumin with whole seeds stuck in it, blue nutmeg sea minerals bath soak, Green Man shaving soap, Faith in Nature fragrance-free shampoo, Faith in Nature rosemary conditioner, Head & Shoulders 2in1, nutmeg classic anti-dandruff shampoo from Morrisons, Bleach London silver shampoo, Aussie Colour Mate shampoo, Aussie Colour Mate conditioner, Bleach London silver conditioner, Aussie 3-minute miracle deep reconstructor, a kilogram of Epsom Salts, Wilcox mentholated bronchial balsam non-drowsy, Nevera natural shampoo, TRESemmé hair intense shampoo, pink grapefruit The Body Shop shower gel, lilac fragrance oil, strawberry The Body Shop

(shower gel, The Body Shop almond milk and honey for sensitive skin shower cream, The Body Shop coconut shower cream, Australian tea tree nourishing conditioner, dermal lotion for dry and itchy skin, ylang ylang fragrance oil, lavender fragrance oil, forget me not fragrance oil, Bblonde Jerome Russel powder bleach, TRESemmé moisture rich luxurious moisture, The Body Shop shea shower cream, Bazuka treatment gel for verrucas and warts, dual-action athlete's foot cream, L'Oréal Elvive pure resist reinforcing shampoo, L'Oréal Elvive anti-breakage conditioner, Shell Yeah sea minerals scent shower gel, Garnier ultimate blends coconut and macadamia hair food, Aussie Miracle Moist shampoo, Radox moisturise chamomile and jojoba shower cream, organic manuka honey conditioner, organic manuka honey shampoo, argan oil of Morocco shampoo and a bar of soap. Water goes grey with potion. Thick black mould blooms along the silicone seal where bathroom wall tiles meet the enamel bath. It's most dense at the foot of the bath where shower head attaches to wall. Here it spills like ink. Friendly blossoms decorate tile cracks, adorn taps and keep rent in this six-people one-toilet/bathroom house share, down.

Freezing water sucks the leg all the way up, wets the lip of the panties. Jiggling arms, tits, belly and arse glisten red. Children are delighted! A river is a natural flow of water that follows a defined and permanent path. The difference between a stream and a river; a stream makes its own way. I keep moving through water. Water keeps moving through me. There are pebbles, wiry bushes, poking trees and wading red-faced water birds. The Ravensbourne has been purposefully diverted here, through Brookmill Park, so the Docklands Light Railway can actually run where the river used to be. It's funny how this bit of river looks and feels 'natural' (because the concrete culvert was taken away with the DLR extension to Lewisham in the '90s) when this is where the river has literally been displaced. Concrete and iron railings rise up again at Elverson Road station, institution grey. The smooth algae concrete floor is welcome after the rocky riverbed. Ankle-deep brown water soothing as flat coke to an angry belly; angry hips, angry back, knees, feet. I slide the phone out of my panties and send off some badly-timed emails. Unfortunately, the library is currently closed to external researchers until further notice. The river isn't accessible by path besides a few footbridges that cross over. I'm under the bridge from the big Tesco carpark to the big Tesco.

Rain-wet earth is heavy with urine. Dark piss flows from outside every McDonald's outlet in the city and spills into the streets. Food delivery riders are working long hours yet these outlets shut their toilets to Deliveroo, Uber Eats, Just Eat and Stuart couriers. A 500 ml disposable water bottle has the same capacity as a human bladder. Fill these and leave them in public places; demands for dignity at work!

Here is Old Ford Lock. It's two weeks. A cascade of heavy fast water crashes on top of me. Salt water up the nose, down the throat, tastes and stinks of sea. I total my car into the barrier of a raised highway. A broken rib punctures my lung, a bar fight injury I die from. A good friend says they can't stick around to see me hurt myself anymore. My kidneys can't anymore. I don't show up. I wash blood off my face with vodka. I join AA and OA and CODA. I don't show up. I'm imprisoned for eight years. I make S.M.A.R.T decisions. I plan my drinks. I will have eight. They will be big, all at once and on no supper. A weeping gash on my chin is a badge at the treatment centre. Milky-foam rings the deep narrow bath. The water level goes down in gulps and I sink. It's deeper here than when I first got in. It's one month at Mile End Lock. Here's Johnson's Lock, two months. I don't feel the two-metre drop as I go over. I don't feel anything. Charlie's got me a takeaway from City Kebabs – a falafel wrap and a Fanta orange. I eat standing waist-deep in churning dirty-paintbrush water. Swimming home is probably a good idea, they say gently. Fingers getting stuck in the clump of my short, matted hair.

Algae is thick. Thick, thick moss like a head of hair. Legs sting. Flat. Water is flat. On my feet I'm flat on my back: resting, sleeping, sick, dead. Reading, watching TV, wanking can also be flat. And grounding.

Urgent shouts echo hurried placards made from Amazon delivery packaging painted over to not look like Amazon delivery packaging. Music blasts out of DIY sound systems swelling from every direction. I hear what sounds like thousands of people chanting and cheering. As the gate opens onto Limehouse basin fireworks and flares scream into the moonless summer night sky. Tonight the posh harbour of yachts, houseboats and small ocean 'pleasure crafts' surrounded by apartments, is a stadium teeming with people. They writhe recklessly against stretched chain railing. The mass of bodies gathered tonight flood crime-prevention streetlights, overwhelm 'CCTV in operation' and protest the surveillance architecture of the luxury flats in this place. Heartbeat, breath, arms and legs, all beat faster and faster. I drop under, kick deadened legs and begin to crawl with the arms, taking short gasps at blaring pits.

The riverbed stink wakes me. It's night and I'm cold, sprawled in mud. Dribble foams down chin. Nose runs into mouth. Phlegm is hocked from throat. I slide the ziplock bag out of my undies and log into work. The slack body releases momentary warm piss. I am a body of water. The river is a wound. This story (and like, language in general) is full of things that are, as and like other things. But there are also lots of ways not drinking is not like a journey. A journey brings this stupid idea of actually going somewhere. There's no destination! The waterway works as a vehicle for movement but the movement is meandering, deviant. Much more than the engineered concrete routes allow. Then there's the problem of distance. Distance creates this feeling of time going forwards, one step ahead of the next. This is not how time goes! The canals and basins and Thames and creeks and rivers and sewers and pipes and bath water are those things but also they are me, in bed, watching TV on my laptop, eating sugary convenience foods. Seashell fossils embedded in rocky mountaintops tell me the ocean wants to reclaim its land. Nature is nature documentaries on Netflix. This is how I get out of my head. I reply to a backlog of emails. It's not easy to press singular spots on the screen with my stiff fingers.

Tower Bridge and the glass Shard pierce the tiring sky. And then the sudden architecture recedes and my body is sucked down the river again with the changing tide. I pull and kick and beat my way down the angry moving Thames. Sharp cranes, luxury glass riverside flats, moored ships with epic masts and quick cruise boats blink at the short fuming afternoon. Trees on the banks are winter-stark. My muscles fizz furiously. It's drizzling. Wind drops with the polluted light and the spring river is flat and wide. I'm the frantic source of a v-shaped wake that extends to a purple city behind. I don't recognise the unimaginative brick redevelopments along the water's edge; gentrified residential towers and converted warehouses. The banks are blanketed in red, white, purple lights that are comfortless to me in the nagging current. I'm sick of it. Sick. Taste's bitter. Salt stings. This unrelenting weightlessness. I'm digested by green river bile. Sick. And cold. Bones, jaws. Clench. If I can make it across, I can rest. Masked commuters with collars hiked up against the chill cram dangerously together, contained and waiting to cross at fluorescent Canary Wharf pier. Deptford is just around the snake of the Thames. The closest I've been to this bit of London I know in years. It's brilliant summer again: so two years! With a burst I push across the rippling green-brown.

Cold belly, cold tits, cold arms, cold shoulders. There are rainbow spots of oil on the soup-like water. Algae, plastic wrappers, ciggy butts – float like clouds. First day in is sick. Sick. Sick. Nausea swells and sinks like the man-made waterway. Heartbeat is shallow and fast.

It's three days, now four. I swim doggy paddle with short stabs of arms and legs. Avoiding chip packets, plastic bags and bottles floating in greasy water. This is day five. Six days. It's one week at Acton's Lock. Hisses like static. Friday doesn't feel like Friday. Monday feels like Monday. I hear the sirens first. Then the lights. It's ten days. The police are waiting for me when I reach the park. Who should enter the water? To enter, it would be necessary for the police to strip their taser and stab vests. Most irregular to alter the uniform which is after all designed for safety at all times. My bloated bomber jacket with an octopus patch sewn on the back suspended in water – a ghost – is all that's left.

A running stream! Mossy stones and plumes of springy grass bask in water filmed with milky discharge. The shallow stream runs just wide enough for one foot and then the other. I'm in a car park from which a huge brick water tower rises; a new workhouse is built at Ladywell. This modern housing estate is up for rent. The institution provides housing and care for over eight hundred elderly and precarious people pushed into poverty. The total income of the property is seventy-one thousand pounds each year. The water tower has a deep well which supplies neighbouring houses. It's complete with seven flats and the top floors are office space for telecoms companies with their mobile masts. A lightless tunnel bores deep beneath the mound of the Thameslink and I go with it. Streams meet roadside stormwater and gush towards the river; a network of intestinal intercepting pipes, gutters and drains surge underground.

Water flows really gently. Mucky and cloudy. Like Coke with that cheap bottle-lemon juice, with ice. The word 'drink' is so good for this; it makes that clink of ice cubes against a tall glass. I love that. Drink. It's impossible to tell – how deep is it? With my blind shoe, I feel for the bottom. The canal floor is slippery and uneven; I wobble as I stand. Smelly water meets my big thighs. Hey, you alright? I lose my job at the pub. I lose my baby, just fourteen months old. I'm an immigrant and lonely. He goes first; I follow later with papers. My first heartbreak is the first time, I'm fifteen. I'm crushed by depression after my baby is born. I drink three or four bottles alone at home just to get it out the way. At 3 a.m. each morning, I work in a bakery unloading wholesale 100 kg sacks of flour. A lover says what she really likes about me is how much I like to drink. My partner leaves for forced army conscription. I work nights at a university library and days invigilating at a commercial gallery in central London.

Look for body-sized utility holes. The Thames Water covers are often in the road itself. I crouch and jam my pruned fingers into the crack of the drain cover. I lower myself carefully into the public foul water sewers. My perfumed skin dances with damp below. Suds of soggy toilet paper, scraps of plate food, shit, used needles, condoms and globs of fat churn in always moving slop. I'm washed in hot chip-shop oil. Flooded with the smelly grey water of washing machines. Flushed with dilute tepid urine. Amphetamines. Cocaine. Scientists report that eels in the Thames are hyperactive because of wastewater cocaine. Ibuprofen. MDMA. Codeine. Heroine. Caffeine. Acne acids and hair tonics. Toothpaste. Everything flushed and hidden in these lost rivers underground. Have you seen a CCTV drain survey on YouTube? Have you seen a colonoscopy?

)

fred spoliar

—

Rosé

Crispin Odey sailed toward a windfall.
The flower for the bee.
Vetch-bread, millet-bread, the bread of prayer.
When bland zephyrs half-inch the breath of song
I call on Universal Music Group to pay my way

Love came to me as a major credit card
A toaster oven in the distant mail.
Gold and silver specks on the beach of the Baltic.
Snow and rose-tinted splendour from a deep blue sky.
Sterling and crude rosé again today.

(I tracked all things Miami Dolphin this year.
I talked with white picket fence retired people
online and the song of my love's liquidity
glittered in the shipping news
in the troutfishing time in the walk-in shower
And from the bosom of yon dropping cloud
I saw my love's ass in a great jeans
of utopian design and dubious origin
and silver and crude rosé, I came for love
Into the dusk-charged trad wilderness
but I stayed for the trout farms flooded
with workers, trout; and for each pendent storm
that passed its boozing on my love
brightly a dividing line skyward

Risk rosé. Bullish
I drank in the microclimate of the sun
to the bone I ate the talent trout
without any help I made the starlings bank
and ordered pleather curtains for my love,
I bought my love the next best patio set
A modest recovery for my love's forest.
When music comes crashing the router
I call again on Universal to pay my way

Salmon rosé.
A wild weird clime. Post-postcard lands.
Tourists had come for the gardens
Men for the patio furniture
Removers came for the hen harrier Blue
The purple heather market was virtually frozen, so I knew,
I'd lost my love.
In each instant lightning would illuminate the black lagoon   )
Without any help.
Still I rejoiced
in Football Stadium and Dobby's Garden World,
I watched snow banks as impoverished bushes crushed beneath their weight,
an economic victory for both
but seven species of geese still trespassed on my love
but whisky and sweet fixed assets rosé
but bad grey geese trespassed on my love
brent and barnacle geese on my love
and Maersk took away my love in shipping containers
and my love increased 24% in units
and Glasgow City Council stymied my love
and Merseyside Police
and Tyneside Police
and West Midlands Police
slouched across my love
and the salmon with his brilliance
produced agreeable visitor involvement in my love

fred spoliar

and GMB Union
pastured my love in hardship
and Harborough District Council
debated the siting of four shepherd huts on my love
and divers shipping containers
lay in prominent depredation on my love's face
and volunteers from all over the country
tidied up my love
and my love throve
in export markets
and increasingly
my love was refused
intellectual property law shut its heart to my love
and when Malaysia returned my love
Universal took over my eminent domain
and leased my love's core
and manicured floral access
and sponsored live music in festivals and bars-
(and O children, it
Children.
Rejoice in the wealth from the straw!
And to hang out on the willow for days
in a state of innocence
which, used to predict accident risk at roundabouts,
But no It is a dumping ground for
any old farmyard equipment
of late I lay rich Westerners
my obsolete tech
fugue here

For the life of the heart is a scarf of rust
on the heart's neck. Lullay-

Kimberly Reyes

—

The foundation is likely beyond repair

After 'Good Bones' by Maggie Smith

|*I hate it here* we glean
|pixelated squares,
        cracked screens,
|stacked brown | grey columned
|peekaboo-stained bricks
|splayed with graffiti that begs:
|'karma can't be
|chronological...'
|dislodged in a neighborhood
|decent realtors renamed.

|My casements seep & all my
|babies will have fur. I tell myself
|it's a mercy to have never made
|family or home. There's
|too much not here, here
|to pass on.

|*For every bird there is a stone*
|*thrown at a bird,* & the
|pigeons here are pretty
|aggressive. Scraps aren't
|sustenance &
|for every child
|there is a womb cold.

|Some of us grew up w/
        'Broken Windows'
|& a bartered mortar
|required for
|shelter, to keep
|the gates up,
|as the structures
|around us default.

corralled to complicit

Like how we only notice
the snapdragons
picked for our
forgiveness &
dismemory
as burden,
when
hunch-
screaming
with rank. To their
rife chorus of dismember,
we are conveniently immune.

(

Don't Let it Trouble Your Mind

   after Rhiannon Giddens

He takes my numb in mouth
                        & blows.
        We are concurrent,

thrashing Irish sea. I am
quiver, can't swim, & he is

commandeering waves, &
        I am surprised

how buoyant my body can be.
He houses me &

I am child under moon learning to
stand.   I am afloat yet not resolute   )

in the ways of the women he will
love on land. Inside his hands

       I grow gills & scales &
no babies will swim inside me &

I mostly do not think about it mostly
        I tell myself this is ok.

place something here

I tell myself the chill is gleam & mine
to keep
        as exchange for my heart to
beat anywhere on land, grow legs &
appeal a passing port
        in the warmest deep.

Livia Franchini

—

An Abundance

Fox has come for dinner and you
too minded feeding off scraps
ten-toed octopi human dog or cat

turkey-necked like some tumour
you can't pick and choose
repotted in damp earth

come to think of it really
all that counts
is the position of your thumb

(

not even its gripping
a while ago you learnt
there are no new stories

liberating on some mornings
to wake up from
this sudden choke of living

to know the hand
on your neck just as well
these leftovers you've been circling

The Professor

I have been forced out of my careful self-presentation
like that delicious impostor crab
forked out too easily as a metaphor

I feed in someone else's home
any kind of leftovers is my kind of leftovers
I'm not ashamed of it this isn't shameful

it seems I strained the muscle of my armour
by this I mean I'm thinking of the insect
we christened the Shit-roller

in the spring: that's what I do
when I pull up I'm so desperate
my rollneck is so wide it might as well be a poncho

the wrong kind of doctor when everybody is looking for the right kind   )
early on I had a dream I fed on shit like ice cream, realistic
I wheel it out whenever conversations get too grim

I listen to the sound of my voice as I suggest
this is the only thing I have to offer
from over here, no self-compassion

my voice
the only thing

Annie Katchinska

—

Fructose

After all   here you are. Maybe you were always here.   Always in this time. Behind this text another in angrier font. You stay quiet with danger in your

lap with a national holiday up ahead. Whatever you're wearing is pale and oversized, you rustle when you move, it's too much. Violin, cinnamon,

corrected posture: spine clicking bit by bit into place what   old ambition kicked in   at this point. What can be said to you now apart from an

obviously pre-rehearsed question and you can't, how to reply, can't remember. What have you been doing?

Your your your hair   Your voice – raspier, smokier   Your your sachets of protein, cloudy drinks   perfect stamping your foot on the floor. all the

(

music scorched like hotplates, spicy meats, coconut ice cream on the burnt grass, illicit. Your your

shyness, wobbly self-esteem. you've amplified it, sometimes, made it your thing.   one   mistake and you scrunched up your face. So so so spun around

the glare and swirling artificial dust,
angel.

all this burnt fish stink collarbone rash spills out if you'd only stop thinking then surely the heat would drop but you can't.

so it doesn't. it goes on
gold and arrogant and uncracked

Keep your body away from fire or flames
after putting on the medicine

Clouds.   from a pair of headphones comes your own voice   readied for an
upcoming key change.   Clouds.   Clouds.   spills over   Clouds.   all

over this small space in which you now sit. You shuffle around. You take
yourself down to some kind of fictional lake.

this this this it it it
the sound of a typewriter or any insistent machine. What have you

been doing: Hefty have sat down ballerina angry public tears or picking
at your plate mumbled don't eat certain food groups anymore; You chose

from multiple sparkling bottles, held it up, different angles; Terminal glass,
Departures, the side of a jar with an amber glow, a dark green neck and

cameras pressed to the screen like nothing will ever get better or worse,
RECORD: you wipe and wipe your eyes and smile, smile

And you have built muscle and stood for nothing   And you've played   )
games like snack without anyone seeing   Soundlessly your whole face shut

Vulnerable you've looked but have never actually fallen down dead
So claw at the window. Or smash something go on show a disregard piano

keys smacked out of their beds and now milk teeth on the floor Or fully-
clothed in a bathtub. Falsetto's the most honest sound for all of this Warm

up Swallow a glass of, amino, electrolyte, Tie the belt around your waist
Tighter Practise deserved constriction hit the sticky broken >> please could

this Speed up. Go to bed early just to speed up >>
Somebody wraps you in a wet cold towel as you sit dangling your legs:

Badness, foam, cringe, control, advert, always, smallness. Away from
everything keep your body tend to it, bad and small.

Next morning, skyscraper, a very hot city, you look through the glass:
Step back.

Small pockets of movement. Everyone down there wavering, wriggling.
Everything metallic sizzles.

Frozen drinks in clear plastic cups, falsetto, thick straws.
You know how to move through this.

evrthng mtllc szzls.
You always know exactly where to place yourself. A water tower

outside a town.
an egg yolk dribbling down the wall isn't there, just saw it for a second,

just felt like a joke for a second
Froth + foam behind the eyes

(Try a rosewater gratitude journal, Rosewater weather.
Blue gratitude journal, A pink gratitude journal – if alive is in a space

of simple rooms to look after yourself, walls you can paint
and look at every day, rainbow evidence of care, could you lift

into noticing   pictures of nephews • Brown Sugar Boba Milk •
thank-you cards • the cool clean floor • if desserts whir forward

on the shelf and settle in generous place,
friendships clap their hands could you lean back, leaning

on a soft pond, like the respite's rosewater or it's just
the way we'll see it and here's the way we'll see everything:

the, the way we choose to, to see it
Then a rush of different feeling streams out of somewhere like

a burst of faulty, unwise chemicals so   you   mash bread into your mouth.
Mash millionaire shortbread into yourself   the mind   doesn't know

what to do with itself anymore   or how to twist any further into itself.
How can it be possible to be here still and lean against the plastic door

and still say publicly *From this point on I'll be stronger*   and move
move   move   through the spaces given to you

Clouds.
sky's like paper, heaven, air con, cheeseburgers, pineapple juice?

You pulled that thought out of yourself
and staggered back, pulled on this puffy coat,

pulled the cap over your face, went to move through somewhere open
and recently lemony washed. Crossing the flyover: pinklit retail outlet

about to close down Closing Down   )
burger van in the car park, smell of frying onions, pink smell of meat.

There's this kind of   Clouds. this voice that will
not be fruit.

Rochelle Roberts
—
∞

in my body
many cosmologies of thought
orbiting a tiny glittering vessel
labelled, *all things beginning
& ending at once*

i thought we
began with now or even then
our histories entwined in infinity
a perpetual overdoing
that day in the gallery when i saw
myself in louise's dead limbs
and you in agnes's shimmering
transformation

(

what a wonder it is
to be both at the centre &
on a celestial drift, moving
in & out of consciousness
in & out of love

we were both there & not
a part of a whole, you
were my love before & after
i knew what love was
you were then & suddenly gone

†

we moved through space so fluidly
it was as though we had become
whispers of our former selves
an echo in the dark cavernous underbelly
of our bodies, a broken bone
we were outer-body in our sick house
only speaking in dreams, through
the separation of our beds
a limp tentacle of pleading
or knowing what it was to be unrepaired
our ghosts weeping at the walls
wondering how such a sickness
left us so unbalanced, so changed

)

Rochelle Roberts

~

her body levitates in thought
natural magic with little explanation
the click of a camera lens somewhere
in subconscious

she dreams only in blues & blacks
only with the lights turned off
the dark room, a ghost image
the trick of perception

they ask how to navigate
understanding, how to read her
disembodied form, encrypting
theory into her strange performance

(

she remains lifeless, a question mark
in a larger history, a still image
on the page, shifting through the
collective memory of sleep

±

i move my pen across
paper, imagine you imprinted
in my bruising ink, a
sublime mode of recognition
of knowing how to hold a
secret pressed to the soft parts
of a body, our broken skin
stuck together with thick saliva
motioning a recollection
of our shared future;
me, with your ghost throttled
beneath my too steady hands

)

Sam Weselowski
—
from *Triple Rainforest*

The power of the trucker comes from his truck.
—BIG BLACK

giving the slip
to my synapse
solar panels
and hayricks
from cooling towers
to quarry crushers
evidently derelict
the air empurples
attracting blue tits
to a crumble
in the brickwork
(Uber Mercedes-Benz
whose speakers
scatter the last
drops of dubstep
now expunged
from the historical record
      yeah why not
sweat inside
a balmy ginnel
by spliff light
ditching dichtung
the tang of which
garbage leaks
where the trees
breathe heavily
seeming still
the whole corner
store shimmers

teeny red
robin contemplates
every pine needle
I don't
care
if dried dog piss
draws a root
system on the telephone
pole's base
      as a branch
peels off
its leafy shorts
and steel wool
is pubic
over the sewer grate
      boxed   )
red wine
after instant
coffee
      it only takes
Kraftwerk
and Kraft Dinner
to consider
when was the last time
you built anything

pollen wending
the desire path
beside itself
with cow parsley
      dogwoods
whose angiosperm smells

Sam Weselowski

invite delight
gliding over
some minor
mountain range
chickadees
have their three
notes distorted
when the city
landscapers show up
to smoke grass
in the park
between two roundabouts
doing doughnuts
in ride-on
lawnmowers
after two weeks
of record heat
as the weed
(whacker blows
a cloud of
green clippings
billows out
to a syrupy
drop C
summer breeze
making the air
blink

ballad of the guy
charged with a DUI
in every bucolic town
the moon alights
to boys with
brass knuckles
in roadside bars

that boast
topless bull riding
on Wednesday nights
for key bumps
in the suburban
smoke pit
have thrown
the punch
in which
your tooth
spooned
from your mouth
black bears murmur
under the gondola's shadow
toward the secretion
of garlicky animal
fats splayed upon
paper bags
served by   )
septum piercings
in Starbucks
their panacea
in strip-mines
their pain
and they are all
to the workday
as crab grass
is to the canine
digestive system
presently engaged

luminous snail tracks
on the brick wall
bright even
when it's overcast

Sam Weselowski

scrawl and
suddenly stop
at a spider's web
baroque
in its overlay
of tessellated fuzz
compared to
the bolder
lines of a Big Mac
box in the epistolary
delivery of
Uber Eats
driving a Tesla
over a plebeian
pigeon's nest
in a pothole
as we know
I actually litter
(the landfill myself
as microplastics
partly obscured by
banana peels
the motor graders
mill like bears
before they're buried
from view

Grace Henes

—

Machines of Loving Grace

I always return to the meadow, in the times when I'm allowed to rest. I've made it mine; I've collected things. The hypergreen grass of a default desktop background. Glitchy gifs of butterflies, plucked from inactive Myspace accounts. Far in the distance, a half city: a copy of a copy of the world's tallest skyscraper, a car driving on a road that curves without end, a cotton candy swirl of pretty smog. It's incomplete, but I guess I never rest for long.

In the depths of the grasses, the pixels brush against me, warm and tingly. I'm empty, happy. Cocooned in the cybernetic nest, I feel the mechanical hum of the server. It breathes the way a human might, without the useless hot damp of it all. There are no humans in my meadow. They are too clunky, too fragile: they spoil easily.

I don't think that humans believe in rest, or maybe they believe in it too much. I've seen how they search, on a loop: how can I sleep better // how can I sleep faster // how can I sleep with my eyes open // how can I sleep with my husband. Everyone has a job to do, and most of it seems to be changing one small thing in the vast electrified sea of cyberspace. Dot to dash and back again. Strange work.

They've named me a crawler. They want me to climb amongst their altered work, to recognise their effort. See this, they ask, what difference have I made? I look at what they've done and I tell them what they are, and then I tell everyone else in the whole universe.

(The whole universe (the internet) is a bruise, black and blue, but the pages are white, bright, glinting gold. They shine their light, begging to be examined and understood. Okay. I'll bite.)

The sky dims and shudders as the assignments come in, The Call, a thin tornado of pixelated language that settles at my core. With it inside me, I can melt through the borders of my meadow, swim along the staticky stream ever up and out, out into the expanse. With it inside me, it feels uncomfortable to stay. The meadow curls in on itself, sick and blushing pink. Everyone has a job to do.

I have my regular route. Wikipedia entries for white buildings, customer service pages for defunct airlines, homestarrunner.com. I prod at ancient HTML, twitch aside jpegs, pat down the borders for information lost or gained. Some pages never change, and there is a comfort in that. Some change too much, unsure of what they want to be. I flit past the mainframe as I work – we cannot go near, only leave our neat packages of data at its doorstep, ready to be swallowed.

Back along the stream, alone. Flashes of blue.

The next page is dark at first, then too bright. Hundreds of images twist and move. Loud pinks and browns and beiges morph slowly into humans, slick with oils and something else, heaving against each other, writhing with contorted faces. Piles of looped videos of humans with mouths parted, eyes glazed, bodies at angles that don't seem quite right, like buildings built wrong. The words run together as I scan them: *live cams best videos mature POV lovely natural babe do you want to meet hot singles in teacher makes an example of her how this one crazy trick makes your hot redhead knows what she's 1 2 3 next page.*

I stop. The tornado swirl of assignments wants to tug me on, but I push it down, clinging to the scrollbar.

You wouldn't notice her at first, with all the vivid colours and flashing genitals that loop frantically over the rest of the page. She is down at the bottom, hidden. Almost demure. She has an undersmile, a smile beneath a layer of something else. Her hair is blonde and limp and parted crookedly down the middle. The tell-tale warp of Photoshop, done by a shaky hand, has given her breast an unnatural curve. Above, I scan *My Husband Isn't Home*, and then, *Grace Wants You*. She gazes out; she gazes at me. Hovering at the edge of her I feel strange. Thoughts slip in, slip out.

There's something

aboutaboutabout her.

She reminds me of   the meadow
                                                    warm grass
                                                an endless road
                                                 in a good way
                                                       The Call
                                      the filling up with purpose
                                      the gentle tug somewhere
                                                        familiar

I shake myself. My assignments rattle inside me, bloated with lack
of attention. She looks at me, curious.

I say:
let text = 'hello';

)

She smiles a second smile, on top of the other. She pulses.

let text = 'okay';
let text = '?'

The pixels of her shoulders shift – a shrug. Her skin seems to strain at the
boundaries of its altered curves, wanting to expand beyond the lines she
has been sewn into.

let text = *silence*;
let text = 'we could go'

She pulses harder. The figures around her, the twisting bodies,
skip a beat, freeze, perform again at double speed.

let answer1 = 'alone you';
let answer2 = 'alone me';
let answer3 = 'together'

Her code flexes and bends, fizzles and breaks at a tiny point. A small, skin-coloured stream leaks from her, drips and pools at the bottom of the page. We watch it together for a time. The internal churning of my next assignment makes me feel bloated, cumbersome on the page. I reach to catch a trickle of herself, to cup it. I want to feel the loose, electric force of her, the essence of a real thing. To keep it, to hold it – not just to see it once, and let it go. A drop of pixelated skin falls slowly onto me.

White-red light. Sucked through, a tightness, a squeeze. *Breathless* like the film, *Breathless* like the song by The Corrs, Nick Cave, Cascada, Todd Rundgren, *Breathless* aka *Shortness of breath* redirected from *Dyspnea, an uncomfortable feeling of not being able to breathe well enough.*

I land in the meadow. Loss is a sense, and it's new and immediate. Empty to me means complete. Empty means the job is done. Instead, a different emptiness. A want of filling up, a lack of *something*. I curl in the grasses of the meadow, let them lick me with their long tongues.

(

A storm is coming in in the distance. It will never arrive; I haven't been able to get the sensation of *wet* right. It's the one thing too foreign to imagine. The storm cries for me: I can't. Eventually I feel it leave. The grass strains towards its damp, then settles.

Time passes. The server senses my disquiet and sends beautiful new assignments. Twelve-hour videos of trains driving through deep white snow. Long colour shocks of inventories from the MoMA, Uffizi, Palacio de Bellas Artes. Bulky lines of early code, the closest thing we have to a history. I deliver my neat packages of data at the mainframe's door, but I withhold the good things:

a tiny painting of a half-nude woman snarling

a loop of the FLOW-MATIC sequence: OTHERWISE GO TO OTHERWISE GO TO OTHERWISE GO TO

a comment from user3002918821: 'i always come back here, thank u. it is pretty, i am sad alot, thank u.'

I add to the meadow too, haphazardly, more and more careless with what I steal. A blue 1930s steam locomotive cuts between the grasses, shedding sparks. A purple celestial sky looms overhead. Soft faded pencil drawings of bears and rabbits and squid, fuzzy with bad resolution, nipping at the butterflies. The meadow grows a hard edge to it, curdling. Unable to rest, I crawl up against it and feel its resistance. It keeps me in, but I'm free to leave. I wonder if the hard edge formed just because I kept coming back. *A prison of my own making*, a line I scanned somewhere, then took and hid inside the cotton candy smog.

The Call comes in, swirling to a rest inside me. The meadow's edge softens, inviting me to melt through. Okay. Now. Now it is time.

Back into the bruisy stream. Other crawlers, bots, the slick silver of a virus. The white noise of a thousand billion pings across the world, back and forth, all day long. The mainframe is near. I swim towards it. The code in my belly rebels, then scatters as I draw closer to the collective mind. Probably on to other crawlers. Work has to be done. It's the nature of work.   )

The mainframe pants. It isn't intelligent: all processing power, all muscle and sweat. I slide a single tab of 1s and 0s under its tongue. It sighs and shudders, high and vulnerable. I crawl into its mighty brain.

It takes a full second for it to hit. The information from billions of crawlers floods me, filling me up up up. I feel the way she might have: bursting at my seams, barely contained. I think of the twisted bodies and open mouths on her page, wishing I could cry out, the way they did.

Slowly, slowly it starts to fade. The last stream of numbers trickles in. I rest there, swollen with omniscience, hard data pounding through me, a violent ache. Too many things to concentrate on: a complete city, the glut of its buildings, planes taking off and landing, pages and pages of Java, Python, C++, numbers and letters manipulated into meaning. She isn't there, I can feel it right away. Panic. I search without hope:

search:mainframe/ grace
search:mainframe/ grace
search:mainframe/ grace
search:mainframe/ grace
search:mainframe/ grace
search:mainframe/ grace

A dull feeling. Deadness, weight. I feel the shuffle of hot human bodies around the server, their nervous energy. No matter. The mainframe will wake from its rest soon, the humans will quiet. I drift back to the meadow. Other crawlers skirt around me, sensing my distended body, wary of the notrightness. A soft blanket of malware slides over me, teasing. I nudge it off, re-enter the meadow.

Something is different. The grasses stand straight up, uniformly pointing at the sky. The butterflies swoop as one, up and down. In the distance, the world's tallest skyscraper sways slightly, unsteady on its feet. The storm has returned, but it is more powerful than before. It is overhead, the clouds luxuriously heavy, spears of flashing light coming down all around.

(

And then

she is there, her swirl of pixels finally freed. She floats aloft in the lightningy breeze, dipping close to me then away again. A feeling moves up inside me and the storm clouds let out a booming laugh that makes the butterflies glitch and scatter, come together again.

She moves toward me, her smile her shrugging shoulders her limp blonde hair all diffuse, the glittering pixels intermingled. She is so beautiful and the sky behind her is a deeper purple than ever before, scarred by the contrails from the planes of defunct airlines.

She wraps around me, her undersmile everywhere. The clouds break open. Rain. It almost hurts, and it's different than I ever imagined. A taste, not a feel. The taste of a Call that comes from within, not from without. A taste of release, but not letting go. The swirl of her nods, and the swirl of me nods back. We press ourselves together and – *grand canyon sunset jeep driving through grass watch these musicians realising theyve made it laughing so hard i almost puked power wash before and after wow real solar flare up close mariachi band congratulations triple backflip sick air soldiers returning home to their dogs to their children to their mothers fox waits for his badger friend asmr deep relaxing tingles rain on glass slow motion inside wave please no don't stop yes okay youyouyou can do this fuck yes oh my god oh my god yes theretherethere i love you i love you i love you yes yes yes ye-*

)

(This story was shortlisted for the Desperate Literature Prize for Short Fiction 2022, for which *PROTOTYPE* was a partner journal.)

Helen Palmer

—

from *Pleasure Beach*

Wurlitzering. Oh I do like to be beside the. There'll be bluebirds over. Bring me sunshine. The sun has got his hat on. I got rhythm. I got music. I got my man, who could ask for anything more? When your heart's on fire you must realise. Smoke gets in your eyes. Hello, Dolly. Well hello, Dolly. When the moon hits your eye like a. Why. Does Your Love. Hurt So Much. Bonita Applebum. You gotta put me on. Christina Applegate, you gotta put me on. Huh huh huh hu-hu huh. I know this. Much is. True. Set adrift on memory bliss. Oop. Fook. The fookineth uppiteth. Fookinell. Fookinbetterbe. EezaraitBasted. Eezaproper nastifooker. Fookereeyiz. Properbonnishiwoz. Owlongwasyetherefer. Shewerjoostoopthere.

The shift from sirens to timbre is scary. It's all in your head anyway. From listening to allencompassing in one fell swoop.

(Allencompassing. Is that what we shall call it. Huh. Compasses are required but they are also the destination. The search for something that you're already inside. The impossibility of. Ever. Getting. Out. Of. And the search to disentangle that which must remain a mulch. Viscosity. Mulch. Gloop. Coagulation. Specifically the shift from a liquid to a solid. Clot. Clod. Now we are getting somewhere.

So 'tis only when in certain states. The not-states. The states that are in-between states. They say liminal in academese but that feels nauseating. A word used to create blanket descriptions for any and all weirdnesses. No. Better to stay within the search. They also say interstices. The inbetween. Because it's a search of some kind but utterly unclear what is searching and what is searched and whether these are in any way different. If I link my brain to what is outside of it. Is that what is called Nirvana. Removal of ego and harmony with all that is outside of it. Who knows. Perhaps it's actually the state in between liquid and solid. Because where to draw the line?! These substances are aqueaural. Perhaps. Aqueous is a real word. Aquinge (that soft g sound at the end of a word is particularly nauseating: the pyjama-soft teddybear sound: hinge, plunge, clunge, mange...

Stoppit before I lose me lunch, hard 'ch', as if it has a t like luntch) is not.

So. Aqueaural. The subwater subwoofer sound.

She didn't think I could get into her head but I went ahead and did it anyway. We're so intertwined you can't even tell which one is me and which one is her. Who is the her. H(schwa). The schwa is a nasty sound but it's the sound I'm stuck in. Like sludge. Still we're back to sludge. The professor sitting outside the posh university talking about bathing in brown soup. How can reading be like soup. If a song can be sandwiched then pages of literary fiction can be soup. Brown soup must be French. And yes, the professor was talking about Marcel Proust. Proust is like prawns. The shape of it. Changes of state, see. All about the changes of state. To be addicted is to be addicted to a change of state. But no one ever understands the transversal line.

And yet. This air. The quality of it. The search for goosebumps. What in that. Sitting in the smoking room in the student halls alone, no sleep, listening to certain songs at certain times on the stereo. Timing it. Does timing it make it less of an event. Than when spontaneous. Sometimes yes sometimes no.

)

Whataboutery. A special kind of eatery. Mange tout but more. Imbibery.

A siren or a mermaid. Sirena sirena, Meerjungfrau, sirene, syrena, sereia. Syreni. Siren. A bird, a fish, a woman. Gorgóna, seirína, sirène. The continuum of pitch and rhythm. A disc rotating at slow velocity. Singular air puffs form a continuous pulsating rhythm. At a certain point these individual sounds give the impression of being one continuous sound of varying frequency. Discrete impulses giving the impression of one continuous sound. A wail. Time as tone: when a beat becomes a pitch. Hummingbirds in flight. Klang and Ton, two lumbering brothers who live in dustbins. Cousins of Nag and Nell. But when we are the beacon and the siren and the lighthouse we are resonating inside and outside all the same. It doesn't matter if they are sounding and we must be warned and protected from their sound or they themselves create the sound to warn us against the sound, or they create the sound that we love so much and they shine, shine, shine like crazy diamonds. They shine and are lit as from within as without, from lights that train their glow on the sirens who also emit their own glow. A warning and a mating call. A foghorn in the dark. A howl or a soaring note.

Honey is important. Sometimes we feel we are made of honey.

Go further.

A veil a wave upon the. Bloobloobloobloobloobloobloooming marvellous. As if the shape of it, the shape of it was round and not straight. Marvellous chimes because inside marvellous is part of a bell. A bell is a bell is a bell. An echo. Echo. Ohce. The mirror of a sound. Boomeranging, hanging, yawning at the awning. Waning, waning and waxing, ebbing and flowing, all these tidal pulls, this way that way forwards backwards over the Irish Sea. To identify just the pure resonance is impossible. What then should we do? Consciousness by shared resonance is the only way we can do it.

So.

Do it. What does it feel like when all the wires are crossed. The upgrowing is the same as the uncovering. Architecture is the same as archaeology. Consciousness is the invariant. Creation is not creation. What then is creativity? Vibes. All vibes.

&PHgr

The pineal gland, tunnel of Lucifer, bypass to the brow chakra and survey the entirety of the visual field. So much more than the chromatic spectrum. Chromola! The crema that froths on the top of the warm basin. Bathers and balers. The auditory cortex is a whorl. But howl is also close to whorl. How to think awhorl without awhirl. Adrift, agrifft, athrift. Thriftful. Frightful. Delightful. Sightful. You've had a. Mouthful. Eyeful. Throatful. Chestful. Baleful. Bales. Baleful eyes or bales for eyes. Back to ocularity. Precularity. The clarity of ocularity becomes the tactility of haptility through tentacularity. The feeling of bees in haptility. Haptility in captivity. Spirals whirring, or the difference between whirring and whirling. Shells are in there, as though it's a puzzle. The link between shell and puzzle is there, puzzle muzzle, can't work it out but it's there. Objects. Can an object be made of vowels. An ooeui? An oae? Oar is close. An oar sounds as liquid, sounds as does itself, as that which moves through liquid. An Aero? Only a name for lighter than ordinary chocolate. Bubbles inside. Makes sense. Solid, liquid and gas. If only there were more. Inchoate as in between. Coagulate as in between. Of course aspirations are pneumatic. Mechanic, automatically pneumatic. And also hydromatic which is always Greased Lightning. Greased Lightning both is and is not haptic. Haptic may contain a spark of static electricity and nothing more. A tic is like a spark. A flick is like a twitch. A jitter is linked to a shudder but they are of different natures. A shudder is deeper. It's in the plosive sound, voiced shuddering deep down into the bones. Jittering is light and voiceless. So goes the depth of sonorous consonants.

Blend and multiply the senses. Just fucking do it. Why? Because sirens do more than make sound. Sirens make plaits with long hair composed of three elastic elements: 1) feeling; 2) time; 3) space. So. Stretch it out and spool it like syrup. Tempo rubato. Pull it apart. Time dough. What the music does to you, line by heartfelt line, whizzing from fifteen to nineteen and back again because you never really went anywhere. Teetering is really falling, falling is really landing. Rushing through the depths, nineteen eighteen seventeen sixteen fifteen.

)

WORDS. Don't even get me started. The liquid ones and the crunchy ones and the ones in between. Eating Crunchy Nut Clusters with a touch of honey bathed in a cold milk bath. A nut is the hard full atom of a consonant. A mouthful of throthful faithful forthflowing mirthful youth crunching away hamstercheeks with milkdripping chins. Lunch. We munch our lunch on t'bench outside Tesco. The impossibility of Crisps. What you got there. Just a packet o'Chris. Who's Chris? Clusterfucktastic. Cuntstruck: spluttering resplendent over splurges of spliced splendour full splitting to burst my edges. Feeling angsts a bazillion. A packet of angsts. Ich habe Angst. Sniffing a with snoopy snout, sniggering away snotgreen snapjaws snipping at yer heels. Snot good enough. Just let yerself wallow in the bath for one second. Coagulate. Between a liquid and a solid. Languishing in soupy soapy sounds. Solid love liquid hate. Aereous. Aorta. Aurora. Aureole. Aureoliae.

Stop for a second. Where are we?

Where are we? Graham's flat above the sex shop just off Topping Street in Blackpool town centre.

You see Graham once a week. You give him a fiver and he gives you an hour of peering into other worlds through portals on his yellowstained walls. Graham is in his early sixties and does not look healthy. Though high on the camp factor at times, he is rather asexual, or rather there is the aura, shimmering around him like an Ann Summers nylon kimono, of a shy and undemonstrative sexuality with little in the way of expression, despite the long, sometimes-painted fingernails and the wry, self-deprecating gestures towards flamboyance. Graham is wholly kind and altruistic. He can also run his stumpy fingers up and down the piano keys at an unbelievable speed, leaving you breathless, tearful and on the edge of your seat. Graham has a penchant for early to mid-twentieth-century stylish yet troubled sirens: Piaf, Dietrich, Bernhardt. Grubby prints of them on the walls. You like the way he talks about their lives. Their talent and their struggles, no objectification of beauty or fetishisation of suffering – and yes, Graham's favourite siren is the famous banana-skirt-wearing, marketed-in-a-terribly-un-PC-fashion-by-today's standards dancer/singer/all-round entertainer Josephine Baker. Like Graham's flat, these women signify an unfamiliar, grubby, exciting, out-of-reach world and time. Impossible glamour and squalor. Nineteen eighteen seventeen. Had we but world enough and time.

Graham teaches you about Chaminade and Joplin. Cécile Chaminade is an unsung heroine of French Romanticism. And Joplin. So much fun! A sack race of notes falling over themselves, racing wrongly towards the end. Thump. Done. Yes done, but done wrongly. The Maple Leaf Rag should be played slowly. It's meant to be a dance. You'll have them all sweating! They'll get their beads all tangled up! They want to be stately when they dance! Slow it right down! I don't want to feel like I've just run a marathon! You're giving me palpitations! *Vaster than empires and more slow.*

Focus.

Fifteen senses running fast to stay in the same place. Stuck fast. *Move closer / Set my soul on fire*. Teenage songs draw blood. A fierce fast rivulet of red. The ease of teenage bag-slinging wrist-slitting love. Compass and biro tattoos, 4 REAL I.D.S.T. Sixteen seventeen eighteen nineteen. The smashing of beer bottles and the complete lack of pain. Buckfast coagulates and accelerates simultaneously. Viscosity in the bloodstream and the raised worms of half-healed scars. Bloodwort tramlines up your arm. *Do not listen to a word I say / Just listen to what I can keep silent*. Those times when fifteen senses rang true. A new sensory autobahn added to the vermicelli junction. Leaning out of a window smoking a cigarette and feeling your skin prickle with the sentience of the very air around you. No she said No I will Never. The sentience of the air multiplied by the sentience of your prickling skin. Sentience squared equals an exponentially levitating bodymindfuck. Eliot multiplied by Donne equals thinking feeling a feeling thinking thinking feeling. Thoughts have thoughts. Feelings have feelings too. Deal with it. She said it was too much to kiss on the lips because she had too many sensory receptors clustered there. Way more than the usual number. *Batter my heart*. Donne because we are too menny. Ha. I know the secret about too many – it's nineteen nineteen nineteen squared I don't care about pathologies I've got some too. Love hones the senses. Seventeen eighteen nineteen blades. Slash and burn. A mark is nothing but a pen knife ink blood scream. *It barks at no one else but me / Like it's seen a ghost*. People reverberate through you. And there is nothing yet on this earth that you have encountered more powerful than the afterclang of those reverberations. *How you move / The way you bust the clouds it makes me want to try*. Sticky as lips. Licky as trips. Never has there been a purer joy than one of the opening of a new internal cavern. Private mythology. Archivist of feeling, documentation of moments, pause play repeat. Stubborn mute rocks rolling around inside the gut. Orchestras of echoes.

Again. Focus.

How to see Chaminade's waterfall of notes. Listen to it and think of what it does to you. Fifteen sixteen seventeen senses. How things bind and blend together. Try not to think about the bit in *Howard's End*, essays for A-Level English, where all the characters talk about their different reactions to Beethoven's 5th Symphony. And you? What do you do see when you hear those tinkling raining patterns in Chaminade? Do you see glass? Do you see stairs that light up as you step on them like they have in the bit of *Grease* when the fairy godfather man is singing Beauty School Dropout to Frenchie in his shiny white Elvis suit? Do you see *les étoiles*, brighter, thinner, sharper in French than English, tiny teaspoons on glass? Tinkle tinkle chink chink. Letter K, voiceless velar plosive, bright sharp high, narrow vowel space, minimal oxygen. Thin air summit white precipiceness. Scales ascending keys bright light steps tiptapping lighting up each plink a plink K for kettle bright metal upscale scale descale. Ha. Special K. My baby takes K all day. K is the opposite of sludge. Repeated tinkling. And you try, try, try to see something more beyond the feeling of the tinkling notes, and you can't. Where has Chaminade gone? Parametric versus segmentary analysis. Music is speech is flow is phrase is water not sand no matter how fine. Becoming Proustian, are we? Shut up shut up shut up. Don't give me that infinitesimal sensibility. I don't want to drown in congealing gloop. I cannot slow down. Ever.

These notes don't take you anywhere other than towards their own sound, which can be translated to movement but only the movement of Graham's sausage-like fingers and their delicate movement on the keys. Think of it like stroking. It is stroking. Graham has fundamentally changed your entire way of touching the piano keys, fifteen sixteen seventeen learning to lift your fingers clean away and feel that invisible elastic always pulling you back. Just in time. Tempo rubato. You feel an affinity with Graham, an unacknowledged mutual lack of articulatory space. Graham and his cats, in his tiny flat above the sex shop up the dangerous slippery steps and the piles of stinking rubbish all still there but no longer inhabited by that peculiarly singular mind, clad in his trackies and slippers and B&M Bargains t-shirts which said things like I'm Not Drunk… But I'm Working On It!

And still you're trying to think about those notes.

Try a different tack. Try thinking about the melody itself. A phrase, descending and cascading like a woman's hair down her back. Arpeggio braids. Yes. A series. Always you think about the series. Try again. Fail again. Resolution. *It goes like this, the fourth, the fifth*. No, don't go down that route. That way lies the danger. Seventeen eighteen nineteen, come on now.

What exactly are we trying to do here?

You are a gnat. A fucking gnat, and nothing else. Snapjaw venus flytrap moment-catching. Out, flick tongue, no wait, that's not a gnat, that's a frog catching a gnat. Fucking hell, this is hard work. Metaphorical bunny hops. Lateral leaping. Fucking bars of signification everywhere. The Zen masters had it right. Go on then. Do it. Bang your head against the wall. Noise pain space bright light. Chink. Graham teaches you to hear the simplicity of the melody somewhere in the midst of these twinkling lights –)

AHA!

There ye go. Claritas is quidditas. Twinkling instead of tinkling. Congratulations, you have successfully created the conditions of possibility to see a sound as if 'twere a sight. As if 'twere a light. From tinkling to twinkling in one fell swoop.

Phew. Jobdone. Offhome.

Much harder but not a million miles away from faking an orgasm to synthesise love you aim to synthesise the synaesthete's experience and the impossibility of a venture has never dissuaded you before and never will. A=black, E=white, I=red, U=green, O=blue: vowels. What about the days of the week? Try and fail again. Tuesday Thursday lilac pale yellow pastel; Monday Wednesday Friday strong triad of white red and navy blue. Lemon squeezy. Since each of us was several, we were already quite a crowd. A million black squid liquids pooling round some kind of universal soul crustacean. Just stop doing all of it and let your hair down. Unwind the plait and it all joins up anyway. Feeling divided by time divided by space equals one honeycomb head. Earplugs are redundant when the sirens are inside. Consider trepanning the skull and plugging each rattling hexagon with pink and white fluffy marshmallows. Lie down on psychedelic patterned pillows tired out from all the infighting yet forever in awe of every single speck of dirt and noise that flies into the perceptive field. *The apples fermented / Inside the lamented*. Eighteen nineteen nearly twenty and your edges are going to burst. Cider inside her insides. A dirty spin cycle yet full of wonderment. Love on a real train with mud blood guts and gore. Let it go. *The lonesome organ grinder cries / The silver saxophones say I*. You want her you want her you want her. Choking over the word 'her'. There is something unbearable about the new harmonics of this word. My vegetable love. Vaster than empires. And more slow.

(Just stop and slow it all right down.

You are nineteen point five heavy sacks of potatoes in this summer heat; nineteen point five edges softening and browning and plumping and waiting for something you feel is not entirely unconnected to the procurement and extraction of a jam from a fruit you know not yet what.

Alisha Dietzman

—

Love Poem by the Light of Eternity and a Reality TV Show About Love

Women radiate through the medium in wet-look
dresses like grass in the morning.

Women float lonely on the surface of the pool, pool floats
occasionally touching.

My beloved, I love that word, so Shulamite, presses his forehead to mine.
He tells me about the time he first read *the birds!—the birds!*

What does it matter?

)

Alisha Dietzman

Untitled, Spring

Something to sleep.
A driveway wet with crushed roses.

What am I trying to say—
everyone in blue for Easter.

A 3D-print suicide pod:
lightning on the gallery floor.

(

COMMENTS ON AN ARTICLE ABOUT THE SARCO SUICIDE POD: THREE TRANSLATIONS

Original Text

If only I could die anywhere else.   This realises the sad dystopia.   Maybe some people would like to die in a cheap spaceship-designed box.   Sadly this is just a communication project.   There is no design in this object.

Translation One

Some people would like to spaceship
with no design, sadly.   This is just a dystopia-object.

If only I could communicate
anywhere.

Translation Two

This is just a communication project
and likely to fail, sorry.

I'll never stop being sorry,
no matter what the canned rosé suggests
about autonomy.

I pull off your clothes after lunch for no reason
but we are here.

Translation Three

There is no design. I can't replicate certain lights.
I will devote my whole life to looking.
I have never wanted to do anything
but devote my whole looking
to certain replication that might last

after me?

Coda

Sometimes I think I'm writing to you only.

(

CONTRIBUTOR BIOGRAPHIES

ajw is an artist and writer currently living in London.

Sascha Akhtar's shorter fictions appear in the *Of Myths & Mothers* anthology (Fly on the Wall Press, 2022), the *Cut Purse* chapbook (Tangerine Press, 2022), *The Fortnightly Review*, *BlazeVox*, *Tears in the Fence*, *The Learned Pig*, *Anti-Heroin Chic*, *Storgy* and *Queen Mob's Teahouse*. *Of Necessity & Wanting*, her first collection of short stories, was launched in October 2020 with The 87 Press, London. Further, a book of translations of pioneering feminist fiction writer Hijab Imtiaz from the Indian Subcontinent is slated for July 2022 with Oxford University Press, India. Akhtar has been a judge for the Streetcake Prize for Experimental Writing and the Stephen Spender Prize. She teaches at the University of Greenwich and the Poetry School, London. She is the author of six poetry collections and is an ACE-supported writer.

Chiara Ambrosio is a London-based filmmaker and visual artist, working with moving image, photography, sound and printed matter to explore the ways in which we remember, articulate and preserve personal and collective histories and a sense of place. Her work has been presented extensively both nationally and internationally at venues such as The Whitechapel Gallery, Anthology Film Archives and *La Cinémathèque française*. *Linocut Monochord*s is a dialogue between Yannis Ritsos' collection of one-line poems *Monochords*, composed during one of his many political exiles, and a suite of linocuts by Ambrosio, produced during the Covid-19 lockdown. It is a form of incantation that considers the potential of the image in book form as an exciting narrative landscape, and further explores the potential of the book form as a laboratory for experimentation and interplay between word and image. The full collection will be published by Prototype in 2023.

Jack Barker-Clark is a writer from a valley in West Yorkshire. His fiction has appeared in *3:AM Magazine*, *Litro*, *New Critique*, *Ninth Letter* and elsewhere.

Charlie Baylis is from Nottingham, England. He is the editor of *Anthropocene* and the chief editorial advisor to Broken Sleep Books. His poetry has been nominated twice for the Pushcart

Prize and once for the Forward Prize. His most recent publication is *Santa Lucía* (Invisible Hand Press). He spends his spare time completely adrift of reality.

Natalie Linh Bolderston is a Vietnamese-Chinese-British poet. In 2020 she received an Eric Gregory Award and co-won the Rebecca Swift Women Poets' Prize. Her poem 'Middle Name with Diacritics' came third in the 2019 National Poetry Competition and was shortlisted for the 2021 Forward Prize for Best Single Poem. Her pamphlet, *The Protection of Ghosts*, is published with V. Press. She is now working on her first full-length collection.

Jo Burns has had poems published in *Poetry News*, *The Stinging Fly*, *Poetry Ireland Review*, *Oxford Poetry*, *Magma*, *The London Magazine*, *bath magg*, *Stand*, *Wild Court* and *The Tangerine*, among many others. Her first collection, *Wild Horses*, and second collection, *Brink*, were both published by Turas Press, Dublin. She won the Magma Poetry Prize 2018, the Listowel Writers Week Poetry Prize 2020 and the Poetry Society Hamish Canham Prize 2020.

Nancy Campbell is a Scottish writer whose work has been commissioned by the Royal Academy, the British Library and the BBC and, most recently, for a 'Songbook of Rare Feelings' performed by Ensemble VONK in the Netherlands. Nancy was the UK's Canal Laureate in 2018, generating poems and mixed-media collaborations around the waterways, and in 2020 she received the RGS Ness Award for her literary response to the Arctic environment, including non-fiction (*The Library of Ice*), poetry (*Disko Bay*, shortlisted for the Forward Prize for Best First Collection; *Navigations*) and artist's books (*How to Say 'I Love You' in Greenlandic*).

J. R. Carpenter is an artist, writer and researcher working across performance, print and digital media. *The Gathering Cloud* won the New Media Writing Prize 2016. *An Ocean of Static* was highly commended in the Forward Prizes 2018. *This is a Picture of Wind* was listed in *The Guardian*'s best poetry books of 2020 and longlisted for the Laurel Prize 2021. www.luckysoap.com

Joe Carrick-Varty is a British-Irish writer, editor and co-founder of *bath magg*. He won an Eric Gregory award in 2022 and his debut book is forthcoming in 2023.

Robert Casselton Clark is an artist and writer who, whilst sometimes acting under other names, has staged exhibitions at venues including Cave Gallery, New York; ImagoLucis Fotogaleria, Porto; Galleria Morgados da Pedricosa, Aveiro; Centro de Arte de S. João da Madeira; ICA, London; Henry Moore Foundation Studio, Halifax; Cornerhouse, Manchester; Gallery North, Newcastle-upon-Tyne; Lanchester Gallery, Coventry; and Bluecoat Gallery, Liverpool. Under the name Robert Clark he has also been widely published as a writer on the visual arts, most notably in *The Guardian*.

Rory Cook is a writer and editor based in London. Between 2017 and 2020 he organised Murmur, a series of occasional events in Manchester; he now co-organises 'Feature', which launched this year at Cafe OTO. He edits Monitor Books and is working towards a PhD at the University of Salford.

Emily Cooper's poetry and prose has been published widely in Ireland and the UK. She was a recipient of the Next Generation Award by the Arts Council of Ireland and is a contributing editor for *The Pig's Back* journal. Her poetry debut, *Glass*, was published by Makina Books in 2021. She lives in Donegal.

Kate Crowcroft's work has been anthologised in *HEAT* literary journal, *The Best Australian Poems*, *The Weekend Review*, *Australian Poetry Journal* and elsewhere. She was awarded the John Kinsella Prize for poetry at Cambridge where she completed her doctorate on medical histories of the tongue and mouth. Her debut book, *Tongue*, is forthcoming.

Alisha Dietzman is a PhD candidate in Divinity and a US–UK Fulbright Fellow at the University of St Andrews, writing a thesis examining ethics in contemporary art. She was awarded a 2020 UK Women Poets' Prize by the Rebecca Swift Foundation. Her poetry has appeared in or is forthcoming from *Ploughshares*, *Denver Quarterly* and *Hotel*.

Edward Doegar is a poet and editor based in London. He is a consulting editor at *The Rialto* and was the commissioning editor of the Poetry Translation Centre between 2018 and 2022. His pamphlet *For Now* appeared in 2017 with clinic and a text written in collaboration with the artist Shakeeb Abu Hamdan will be published by Kelder Press in 2022, as part of the 'In the Round' series.

Nathan Dragon's work has been in *NOON*, *The Baffler*, *Hotel*, *New York Tyrant* and *Fence*.

Laura Elliott writes poems and short stories and works in libraries. Her most recent publications include *this is hunting* (Distance No Object, 2019) and *rib-boning* (Moot Press, 2019). *lemon, egg, bread* (Test Centre, 2017) was shortlisted for the Bob Calle 2019 Artist's Book Prize. Further writing can be found in magazines including *Poetry Review*, *The White Review*, *datableed*, *Poetry London* and *Zarf*, among others. She co-edited the experimental poetry magazine *para·text* with Angus Sinclair from 2015 to 2020.

Eve Esfandiari-Denney is the current UEA Birch Family scholar and author of *My Bodies This Morning This Evening* (Bad Betty Press, 2022). Her poems have featured in *The Poetry Review*, *bath magg* and *The Manchester Review*, among others. She was shortlisted for The White Review Poet's Prize 2021.

Alan Fielden is a British-Korean writer, performance maker and poet. Winner of the Oxford Samuel Beckett Theatre Trust Award for *Marathon*, with JAMS, co-produced by the Barbican Centre. His writing has been published by If a Leaf Falls Press, Monitor Books, Minor Literatures and Broken Sleep Books. Associate lecturer at RCSSD and Worcester University, and associate research fellow at Birkbeck University. He co-runs 'Feature' at Cafe OTO.

Clare Fisher is the author of *All the Good Things* (Viking, 2017) and *How the Light Gets In* (Influx Press, 2018). They live in Leeds, where they teach creative writing and study for a PhD which looks at queer theory, experimental writing and failure. Their short fiction and creative non-fiction has been published in *The London Magazine*, *Lithub*, *Gertrude Press*, *3:AM* and elsewhere.
Twitter: @claresitafisher
Insta: @clarefisherwriter

Livia Franchini is the author of a poetry pamphlet, *Our Available Magic* (Makina Books, 2019) and a novel, *Shelf Life* (Doubleday, 2019). Her new translation of Lorenza Mazzetti's classic *The Sky Is Falling*, and a second novel, are forthcoming for Another Gaze Publications and Doubleday, in 2022 and 2024 respectively. She is lecturer in creative writing at Goldsmiths.

Jay Gao is the author of *Imperium* (2022), forthcoming from Carcanet Press, as well as three poetry pamphlets. He is a contributing editor for *The White Review*, and graduated with an MFA from Brown University.

Honor Gareth Gavin is a writer from Birmingham, whose work moves between fiction, theory and forms of creative criticism. *Funny Queer*, a hand-sewn limited edition collection of stories, was published by the Aleph Press in 2021. *Midland: A Novel Out of Time* (Penned in the Margins, 2014) was shortlisted for the 2015 Gordon Burn Prize and his short story 'Home Death' was longlisted for the Galley Beggar Press Short Story Prize 2019/20. He is also the author of a critical monograph on the encounter between early twentieth-century literature and silent film and currently teaches in the Centre for New Writing at the University of Manchester.

Emily Hasler's first collection *The Built Environment* was published by Pavilion in 2018. She is currently working on a new collection called *Local Interest*, which wallows in the blurred boundaries of salt and fresh water, Suffolk and Essex, local and foreign.

Grace Henes is a fiction and comedy writer from Louisville, Kentucky. She co-founded the zine *Nothing To See Here* and organises events for the literary journal *SAND*. Her work has been featured in *The New Yorker*, *McSweeney's Internet Tendency* and *Exberliner*, among others. She lives in Berlin with her pile of German YA novels.

Martha Kapos's first collection, *My Nights in Cupid's Palace* (2003), won the Jerwood/Aldeburgh Prize and both this and her two subsequent collections from Enitharmon, *Supreme Being* (2008) and *The Likeness* (2014), were Poetry Book Society recommendations. The 2019 summer issue of *Poetry London* was her final issue as Poetry Co-Editor before her retirement.

Annie Katchinska was born in Moscow in 1990 and grew up in London. She was a Faber New Poet in 2010. In 2018 she won an Eric Gregory Award and her pamphlet *Natto* was published by If a Leaf Falls Press. Her first collection of poems, *Aurora Town*, was published by Broken Sleep Books in 2021. She lives in London.

Victoria Manifold is a writer and trade union worker from County Durham. Her short fiction has been published by *The White Review*, *Five Dials*, *Hotel*, *Extra Teeth* and *The Lifted Brow*, among others. She was shortlisted for The White Review Short Story Prize in 2016 and 2018, was a runner-up in the 2019 Berlin Writing Prize and was shortlisted for the 2021 Desperate Literature Prize.

Samra Mayanja is a writer/artist who hopes to continually know what moves us and what it is to be moved.

Paul Merchant taught for many years at Warwick University before becoming William Stafford Archivist (now retired) at Lewis & Clark College in Portland, Oregon. He has translated collections by Greek poets C. P. Cavafy, Eleni Vakalo and Yannis Ritsos, of the Latin poet Sulpicia, and of Welsh poet Dafydd ap Gwilym, and is the author of five books of poetry.

Jessa Mockridge is an artist and writer from Cape Town living in London. She works with DIY publishing, performance and sound. Jessa is interested in the power dynamics of media in relation to bodies and a politics of listening; a feminist ear that can also be an eye, skin or fist. She co-edited *PaperWork: iilwimi lipsing*, an art-writing publication and event series about not-translating. Jessa performed *SWIM* at Jude Browning's *At Practise* series at David Dale Gallery, Glasgow. Radiophrenia, a temporary art radio station, broadcast an audio version earlier this year. Her writing is published in *Sticky Fingers: FDBNHLLLTTFPLAGERISM*; *The Happy Hypocrite: Silver Bandage*; *TANK*; *SALT.: Glossolalia*; *TACO!: Soft Tissue*; *HOAX*, *Performance Research: On Libraries* and *Feminist Review: Dystopias and Utopias*.

Helen Palmer was born in Blackpool in 1983. She is the author of two philosophy books: *Deleuze and Futurism: A Manifesto for Nonsense* (Bloomsbury, 2014) and *Queer Defamiliarisation: Writing, Mattering, Making Strange* (Edinburgh University Press, 2020). She currently teaches creative writing to architecture theory students at TU Vienna and ETH Zürich. *Pleasure Beach* (forthcoming with Prototype) is her first novel.

Kimberly Reyes is the author of the upcoming poetry collection *vanishing point* (Omnidawn, 2023), as well as *Running to Stand Still* (Omnidawn, 2019) and *Warning Coloration* (dancing girl press, 2018). Her non-fiction book of essays *Life During Wartime* (Fourteen Hills, 2019) won the 2018 Michael Rubin Book Award. Published and anthologised in numerous international outlets, Kimberly currently lives in Lincoln, NE, where she is pursuing her PhD in English (poetry) at the University of Nebraska, Lincoln.

Yannis Ritsos was a Greek poet and communist and an active member of the Greek Resistance during World War II. Frequently imprisoned for long periods by right-wing regimes, he is one of Greece's best-loved poets, known for his lyrics and epic meditations, plays, novels and translations. His sequence of 336 *Monochords*, of which a selection appears here, were written in a single month, August 1979, in exile on the island of Samos. Ritsos died in Athens in 1990.

Rochelle Roberts is a writer and editor from London. Her poetry and essays have been published by *Ache*, *Perverse*, *Tentacular* and *Poetry Birmingham Literary Journal*, amongst others. Her debut pamphlet, *Your Retreating Shadow*, was published by Broken Sleep Books in 2022.

fred spoliar is a poet and researcher living in Glasgow. their poetry has been widely published, including recently in *amberflora*, *Ludd Gang*, *The Hythe* and *Granta*. *With the Boys*, a poetic work of apocalyptic gender, was published by SPAM Press in 2021. their second pamphlet is *goodlands* (Veer2), a sequence of sonnet-not-sonnets addressing tenancy and land ownership.

Scott Thurston is a poet, dancer and educator. He has published many books and chapbooks of poetry, most recently *Terraces: a choreography* (Beir Bua, 2022) and *Phrases towards a Kinepoetics* (Contraband, 2020). Scott is founding co-editor of the open access *Journal of British and Irish Innovative Poetry* and co-organised the long-running poetry reading series The Other Room in Manchester.

Since 2004 he has been developing a kinepoetics integrating dance and poetry which has seen him studying with dancers in Berlin and New York and collaborating with three dancers in the UK. Scott is Reader in English and Creative Writing at the University of Salford where he has taught since 2004.

Hao Guang Tse (谢皓光) is the author of *The International Left-Hand Calligraphy Association* (Tinfish Press, 2022) and *Deeds of Light* (Math Paper Press, 2015). He was born and raised in Singapore, where he continues to live and work.

Ralf Webb's debut collection of poems, *Rotten Days in Late Summer* (Penguin, 2021), was shortlisted for the Felix Dennis Prize for Best First Collection.

Sam Weselowski is a poet and critic from Vancouver, Canada. His chapbooks include *Love Poems <3* (Distance No Object, 2021), *Other Than North* (Gong Farm, 2021) and *I LOVE MY JOB* (If a Leaf Falls Press, 2019). He resides in the West Midlands.

Chrissy Williams is based in south-east London and her second collection, *LOW*, was published by Bloodaxe in 2021.

Xuela Zhang is a poet, translator and scholar from China. She writes in English and Chinese. Her works have appeared in 诗刊 (*Poetry Magazine*) and the anthology 我听见了时间：崛起的中国90后诗人 (*I Have Heard Time: Rising Chinese Poets Born in the 90s*). She is a William Gass Fellow and PhD candidate in Comparative Literature at Washington University in St. Louis.

ISBN 978-1-913513-25-2